Doodling on the Titanic

Also by Osha Neumann

*Up Against the Wall Motherf*ck*r:*
A Memoir of the Sixties with Notes for Next Time

Doodling on the Titanic

The Making of Art in a World on the Brink

Osha Neumann

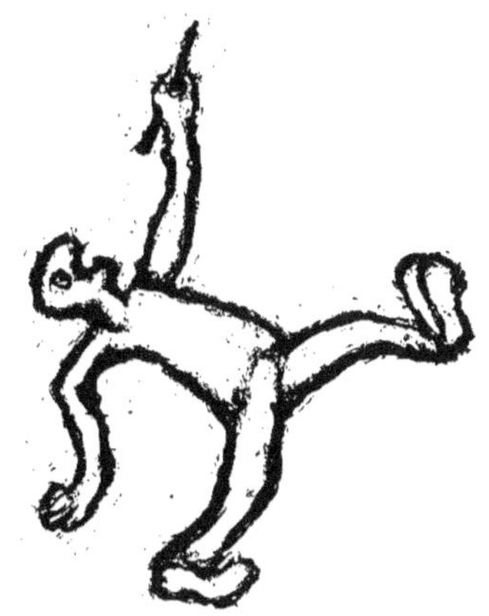

DRAWINGS AND DOODLES BY THE AUTHOR

ISBN 1-978-0-9904969-0-8

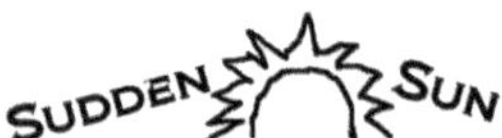

Sudden Sun Press
1840 Woolsey St.
Berkeley, CA 94703

Drawings, doodles, and cover art by the author
Design by Debbie Berne

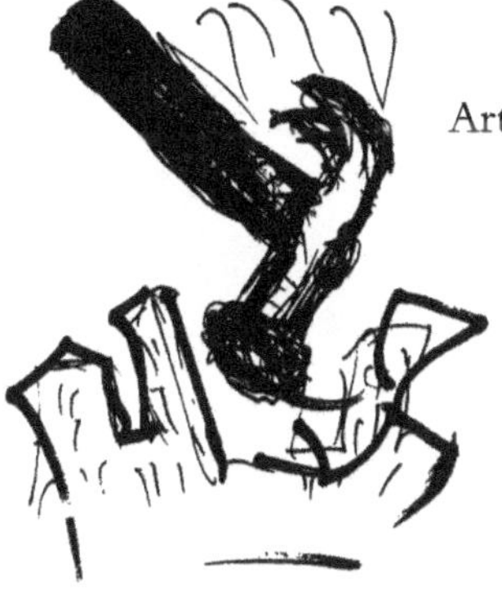

Art is not a mirror to hold up to society,
but a hammer with which to shape it.

Attributed to Bertolt Brecht
(but also to Vladimir Mayakovsky)

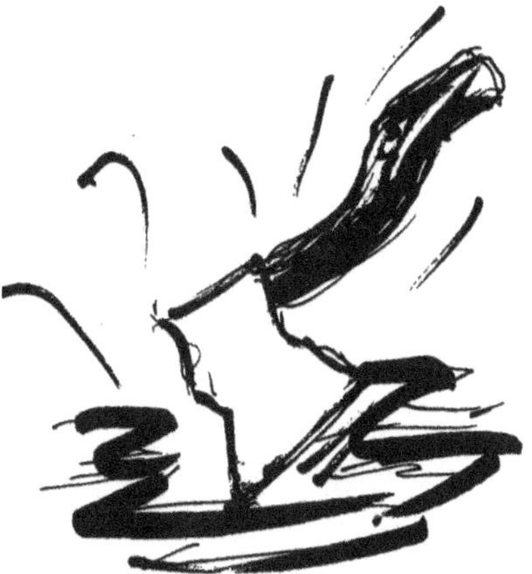

A book must be the axe for
the frozen sea within us.

Franz Kafka to Oskar Pollak,
January 27, 1904

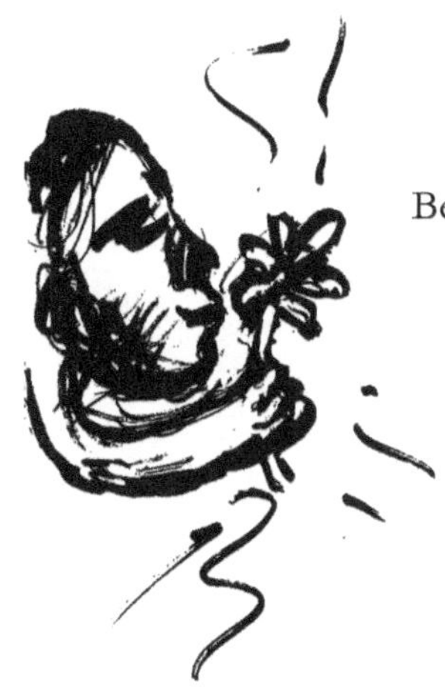

Beauty is nothing
but the promise of happiness
("La beauté n'est que la promesse du bonheur")

Stendhal, De L'Amour (On Love)

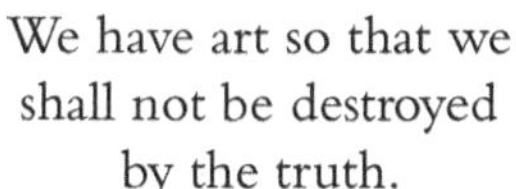

We have art so that we
shall not be destroyed
by the truth.

Frederich Nietzche
(quoted by Michael Ondaatje
in the epigraph to *Divisidero*)

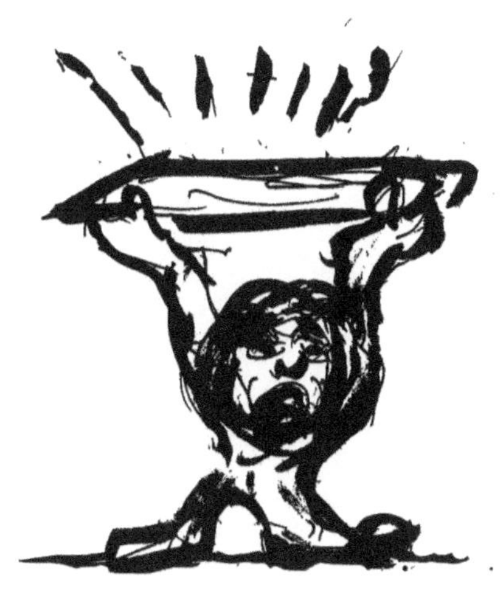

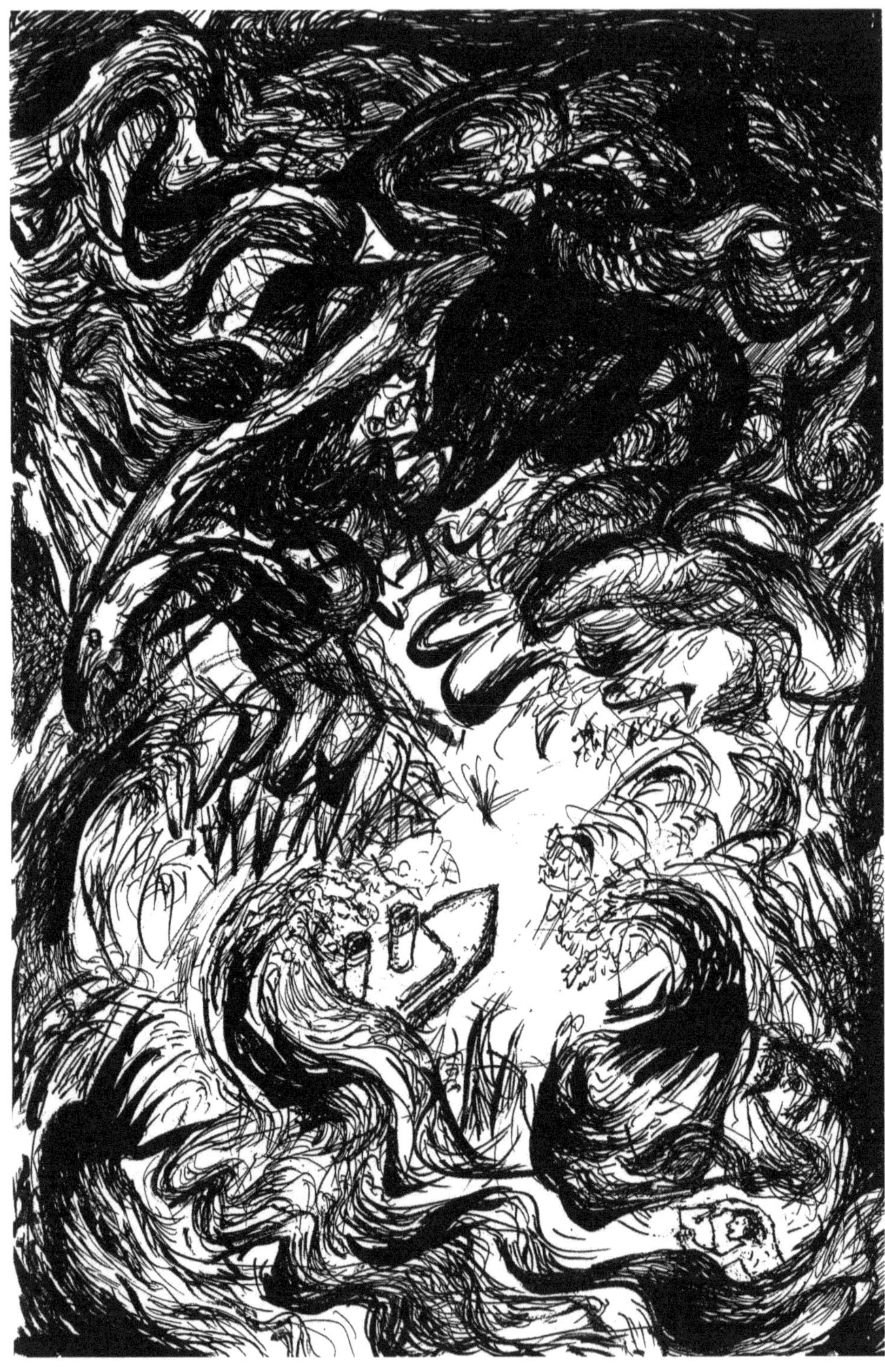

Contents

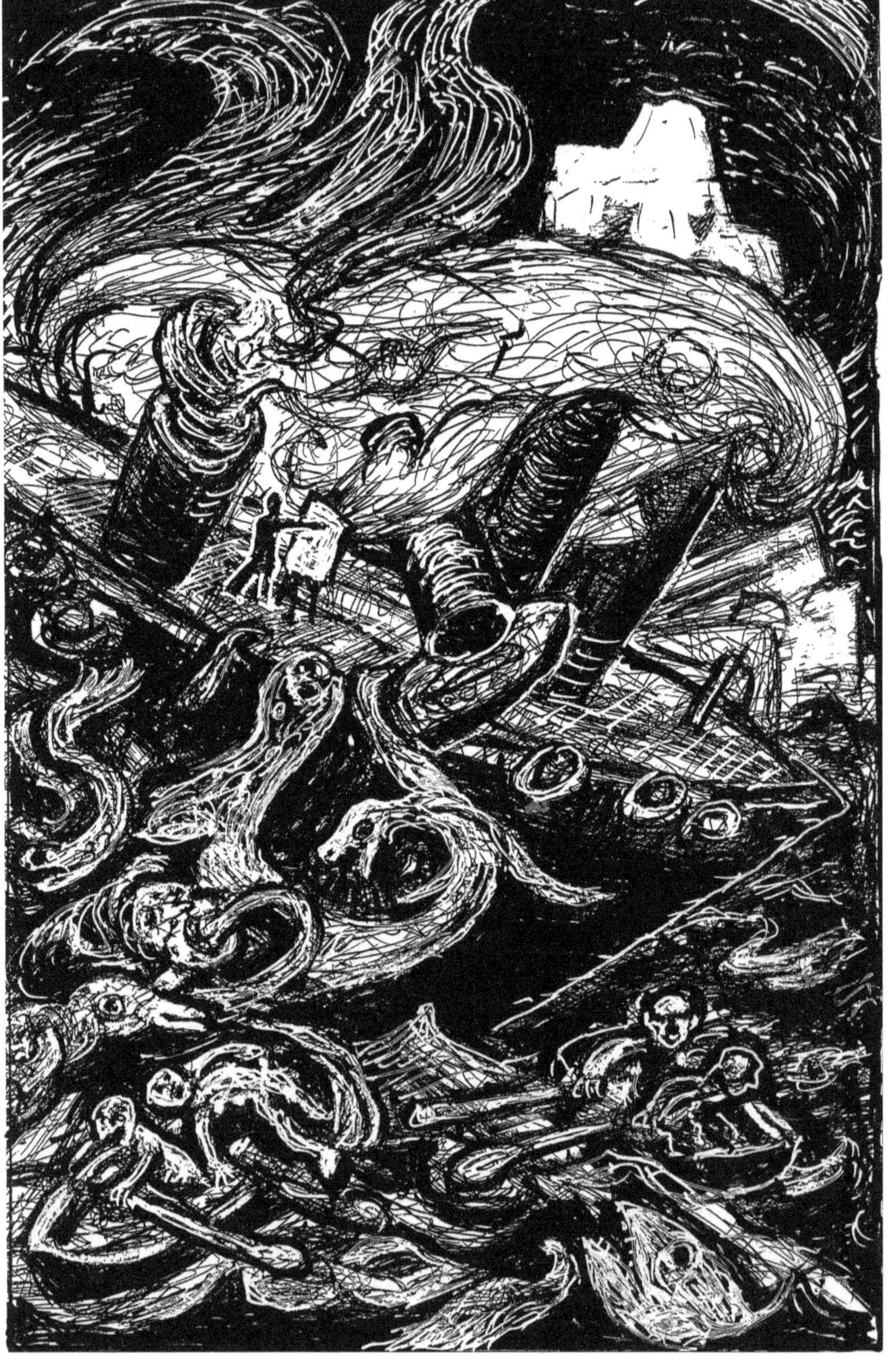

Preface

ART, PERHAPS MORE than any other field of human endeavor, inspires endless streams of blather. A lot of loony nonsense, most of it. What is important about art—its beauty, its truth—eludes explanation. Most writing about art consists either of commentary about what is inessential—biographical facts about the artist, speculations about influences, interpretation of iconography—or verbal gestures toward the ineffable that dissolve into abstruse streams of quasi-profound, pseudo-philosophical speculation. There is no formula for creating beauty. One can describe it only after the fact. What Potter Stewart said about pornography, Immanuel Kant (in so many words) said about beauty: You know it when you see it. And not before. Even where language is the medium of art, its beauty and truth is irreducible to language.*

* Justice Potter Stewart:
"I shall not today attempt further to define the kinds of material I understand to be embraced within that shorthand description [hard-core pornography]; and perhaps I could never succeed in intelligibly doing so. But I know it when I see it, and the motion picture involved in this case is not that."

Concurring Opinion, *Jacobellis v. Ohio*, 378 U.S. 184 (1964)

Immanuel Kant:
"If we wish to decide whether something is beautiful or not, we do not use understanding to refer the presentation to the object so as to give rise to cognition; rather, we use imagination (perhaps in connection with understanding) to refer the presentation to the subject and his feeling of pleasure or displeasure. Hence, a judgment of taste is not a cognitive judgment and so is not a logical judgment but an aesthetic one, by which we mean a judgment whose determining basis *cannot be other* than *subjective*.

Critique of Judgment, trans. Werner S. Pluhar (Indianapolis: Hackett Publishing Company, 1987), 44.

"Aesthetics is for the artist as ornithology is for the birds,"[1] Barnett Newman is said to have said, but, of course, this also is nonsense. Artists are always thinking while they work: *Why am I doing what I'm doing? Is it good? Where does it fit in the vast museum without walls of all the art that's ever been done?* The thoughts are there in the background, half attended to, mutating and multiplying. As far as we know birds do not go about building their nests with a similar buzz in their brains. Artists may not put much stock in theory—the best theory in the world won't generate a poem or a painting worth a damn—but they don't stop thinking. I'm sure Barnett Newman, who studied philosophy at City College of New York before he took up painting, was no exception. Only someone who's ruminated on the relation of thought to art could pronounce so categorically on its irrelevance.

In 1963 I dropped out of graduate school at Yale and moved to the Lower East Side of New York to become a painter. In 1967, as the incandescent insurgencies of the '60s flamed toward their apogee, I gave up painting and became a founding member of an anarchist street gang, the Motherfuckers.* Before I abandoned my paint-splattered tenement apartment crowded with canvases, I began an essay on the end of art. I believed that art had become irrelevant, and that the total imaginative transformation of the world was not merely possible, but necessary. To confine the imagination within the four corners of a canvas seemed to me to capitulate to an intolerable reality that bred ugliness and injustice as carrion breeds maggots. I never finished the essay. Once I made up my mind to leave art behind, I no longer had any interest in elaborating intellectual justifications for my decision.

The Motherfuckers raged in the streets, got busted a lot, wrote thunderous manifestoes—and, in a few short years, burnt out. I did not return

* How, after growing up in the home of German Jewish refugee intellectuals, I ended up in the Motherfuckers, I relate in my memoir, *Up against a Wall Motherfucker: A Memoir of the 60s with Notes for Next Time* (New York: Seven Stories Press, 2008).

to the making of art until almost a decade later when, walking one day in the Mission District of San Francisco, I looked up to see the walls of buildings, two, three stories high, covered with murals that sang with all the color and vitality of the streets. They were the work of Chicano artists who happily ignored the shenanigans of avant-garde art. Here was proof that art could be wonderful *and* popular. It could even—still!—tell a story. It did not have to hide in galleries and museums. I was hooked.

I decided to become a mural painter. *Los Tres Grandes*—Diego Rivera, José Clemente Orozco, and David Alfaro Siqueiros—became my artistic heroes. I offered to paint people's walls for free. I lived off unemployment and put cans for donations out on the sidewalk next to my paints and brushes. When unemployment ran out I applied for grants from the California Arts Council. I painted murals on the walls of gymnasiums and taught art to crazed junior high school students. And then, when there were no more grants to be had, and I faced the prospect of making a living as an artist, I gave up on art for the second time. It wasn't just fear of poverty. It was also a failure of nerve. I had a reasonably realistic view of my talent, and I doubted I was good enough to make a living as an artist. I wasn't even sure I wanted to. Opportunities to paint murals that were not vetted by politicians and bureaucrats were drying up. I had no interest in sucking up to corporations so they'd let me paint their lobbies. And I hated the gallery scene.

I wanted to think and write again. I wanted to find a way to do politics that did not involve running in the streets and throwing things. So I went to law school and became a lawyer who doodles in the margins of his legal pads. I supervise a free legal clinic and represent homeless people busted for doing nothing more than trying to stay alive. Law is my day job, but just about every weekend I sneak off to an overgrown landfill that juts out into San Francisco Bay and sculpt (in collaboration with my multitalented son-in-law Jason DeAntonis) larger-than-life figures of men, women, and animals using the scrap wood and metal I find there.

And at night, after work, I draw—and draw and draw. Using pen and ink and Sharpie markers, I fill sketchbook after sketchbook. Lawyer and artist, I maintain dual citizenship and shuttle between worlds.

The questions I asked myself as I typed away in my railroad flat on the Lower East Side, composing my premature farewell and good riddance to art, remain unanswered: Why does art matter? What is it about a work of art that distinguishes it from all the other stuff that human beings make? Should art take sides in the struggle to change the world? Why does avant-garde art flirt with anti-art? Is art at risk or simply going though its usual changes?

These questions have been with me for a long time, but I feel a need to address them with renewed urgency. We are in the midst of a crisis of capitalism. Whether it is the final crisis remains to be seen. The crisis of capitalism is at the same time a crisis of nature. The biological basis of human life on the planet is at risk. The stakes could not be higher. On the one hand disaster for the human race; on the other hand *the total imaginative transformation of the world.* Nothing less will avert catastrophe. The fledgling movements rising up to challenge capitalism *must* win. And the odds are against them.

Now all that matters today is to seize the helm of history. Time to change course or die. At this critical moment, all human activity, including the making of art, must be judged by its relation to the struggle for change. When a ship is heading toward an iceberg, it's not the time to be painting watercolors. It's all hands on deck. So the question of the relation of art to politics takes on a special urgency. Is art a doodle on a sinking ship, or a bugle call to action? Is it mirror or hammer? Neither or both?

Sometimes scientists find that the study of simple life forms provides insights useful for the understanding of more complex organisms. Following their practice, I begin my effort to understand what art is doing and where it's going by looking at the simple act of doodling. I then go step by step through the making of a drawing and move from there to address the big, devilishly difficult questions that have troubled me so long.

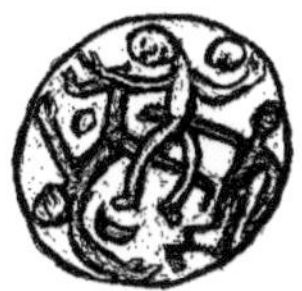

IN WRITING ABOUT ART, I have not felt a need to argue. I've also avoided credentialing my opinions by citing well-known authorities who agree with me. With one exception. Herbert Marcuse was a close friend of my family and colleague of my dad. He moved in with us after his wife died, and after my dad was killed in a car accident he married my mother. He is also, it turns out, my biological father. I remember talking with him about art when he was writing *The Aesthetic Dimension.* My ideas about art grow out of my experience making it, but they undoubtedly also reflect his influence. For those who are curious, I include a brief discussion of his ideas in an appendix.

I owe a huge debt to the wonderful artists with whom I've worked over the years. The murals I have painted and the large sculptures I've made have been collaborations. I have had the good fortune of working with artists who are far more talented than I. O'Brien Thiele is a remarkable painter and a tender, self-effacing friend, who has over and over taken the crude figures I'd drawn in a cartoon for a mural and turned them into something true and beautiful. Jason DeAntonis takes for granted a jaw-dropping talent I would give my eye teeth or some other suitable part of my anatomy to possess. I'm embarrassed by the number of times I've accepted credit for sculptures we worked on together, when the majority of credit should go to him.

When I gave up painting murals, I couldn't see my way back to making big art. Then one day, Jimbow the Hobow took me for a walk. He was living at the time on an overgrown landfill that jutted out into the water from the eastern shore of San Francisco Bay. He showed me the work of Scott Hewitt, David Ryan, Scott Meadows, and Bruce Rayburn, who collectively called themselves Sniff. Like inspired madmen they had painted wacky, bawdy murals on the enormous slabs of concrete that had been dumped along the shore. Inspired by them, I started making sculpture for the first time in my life. Their work at the landfill is long gone. David and the two Scotts continue to paint marvelous paintings together, reminding me that whatever my head says about the future of art, it's the artists that lead the way.

Finally, to Luna and Plum for your effervescent creativity, to Rachel for sharing the excruciating pleasure of writing, to Arisika for giving me reason to believe in the possibility of happiness, to Diallo and to Emma and John and Yeshi and Gus, to all of you for being family and helping me feel human—vast heaps of gratitude.

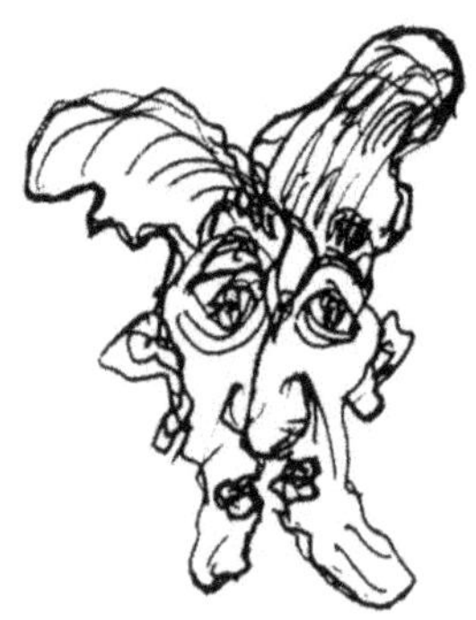

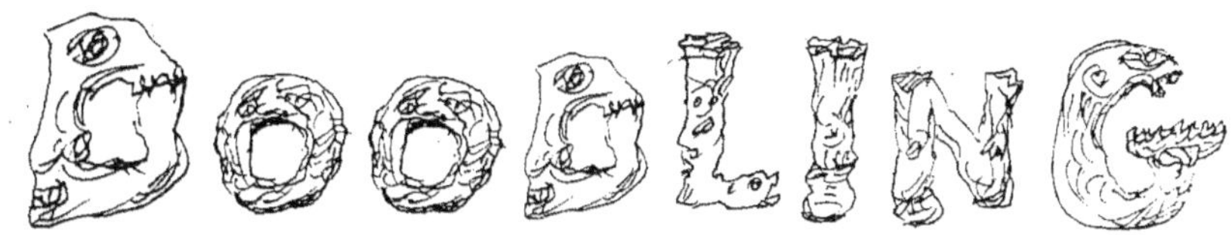

I AM AN INVETERATE DOODLER. I am incapable of sitting through a meeting or listening to a lecture unless half my mind is otherwise occupied. The problem was particularly acute in law school. There are precious few pictures in law books. The law drives the mind away from fluid sensuous experience toward abstractions. Doodling was my way of staying in touch with all those layers of mind that the law considers irrelevant. It became an obsession. I engraved doodles in styrofoam coffee cups. I doodled on napkins. I doodled all over my notes.

"Doodle." The very word is ridiculous. "Noodle," "doodle," "kit and caboodle"—those double "o's" are a sign of silliness. Doodling is an activity of no consequence. It's a sideshow, a semiautomatic act, a *thoughtless* act. I'm supposed to be paying attention, but my mind wanders. My ass itches. I'm bored, I fidget, I have a sexual fantasy or two. And since it's not polite to scratch, and I can't fulfill my fantasies, I doodle.

The problem for serious doodlers is that doodling tends to move from the margins of our consciousness to center stage. The doodle demands attention. We care about it. A curved line requires an answering curve. An unconstrained squiggle asks to be enclosed. A face demands ears, eyebrows, and a grin. The doodle expands, spreading out from the margins of our notepad into the notes themselves, and we realize, perhaps too late, that we haven't been listening to the lecture and have no idea what people are talking about in the meeting.

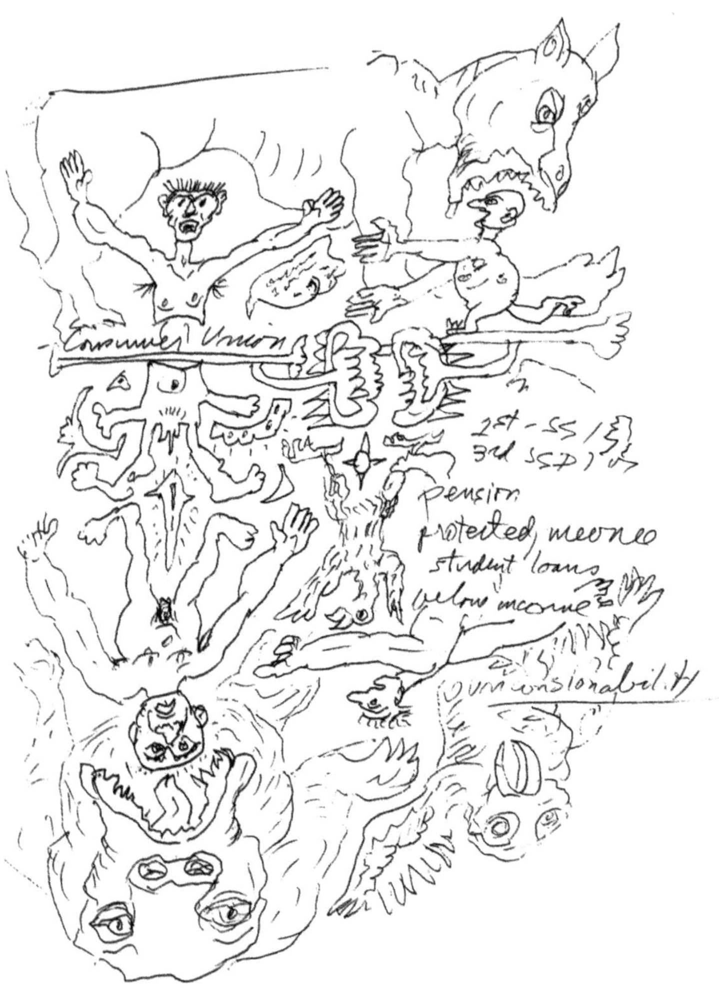

When we examine the very first sketches that are the germ of great works of art, they often look very much like doodles. We see in them the artists groping for form in the abyss of freedom. To find those forms, the mind must be allowed to roam on a loose leash.

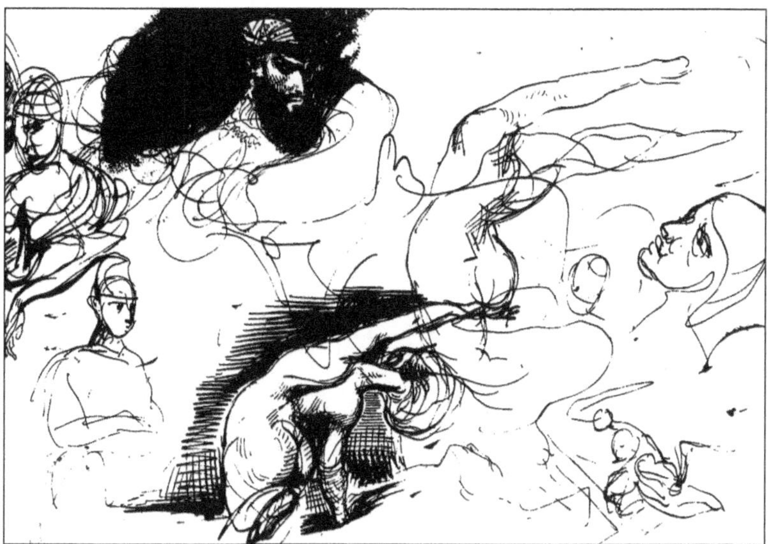

Eugène Delacroix, studies for *Death of Sardnapaplus*

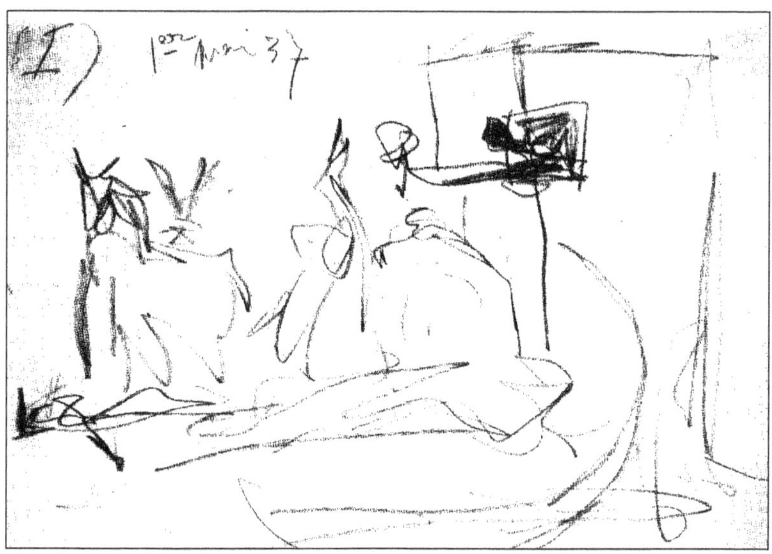

Pablo Picasso, first preparatory sketch for *Guernica*

No sharp line divides the doodle from the work of art. Artists doodle, and the doodler who loves his doodles may decide to frame them and hang them on the wall. Doodling and the making of a work of art happen in a realm that is free from the obligations and necessities that dominate our waking life. What distinguishes the doodler from the artist is that the artist sets out with the intention of entering this realm of freedom—enters, so to speak, by the front door—while the doodler slips in the back way, when her conscious mind is otherwise engaged.

Doodles and works of art are products of a realm of freedom that opens up inside the realm of duties and obligations. The workaday world demands activity governed by thought. Art and doodling are "thoughtless." They do not obey the logic that structures conceptual thinking. Their logic is a logic of forms, whose rules are reinvented and rediscovered with each line drawn, each color laid on the canvas, each stroke of the brush.

Sometimes I doodle and sometimes I sit down and decide to draw a picture. For me the distance between mindless doodling and mindful drawing is not great. I'm sure there are artists who have a firm idea of their final destination when they set out to make a work of art. I seldom know where I'm going when I begin.

I have a poor visual memory. I cannot call to mind the look of things. My imagination is nearly blind. I've tried over and over again to learn the anatomy of an arm, the spatial relation of the biceps to the triceps to the brachialis—and failed. If you asked me to draw a horse or a dog or a cow I can only draw something vaguely mammalian. By dint of enormous effort, numerous false starts and erasures, I claw the forms of things in the world out of a squiggle of lines and blotches.

Undeterred by the quirk of fate that I love something for which I have little natural aptitude, I continue to draw and paint and sculpt, lucky to live in a time when facility at representation is no longer required and signs of the struggle for form are valued in themselves. I wrestle forms out of the void, out of chaos and formlessness.

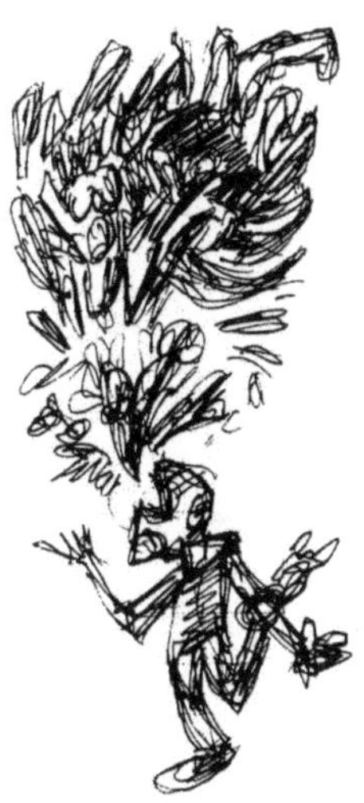

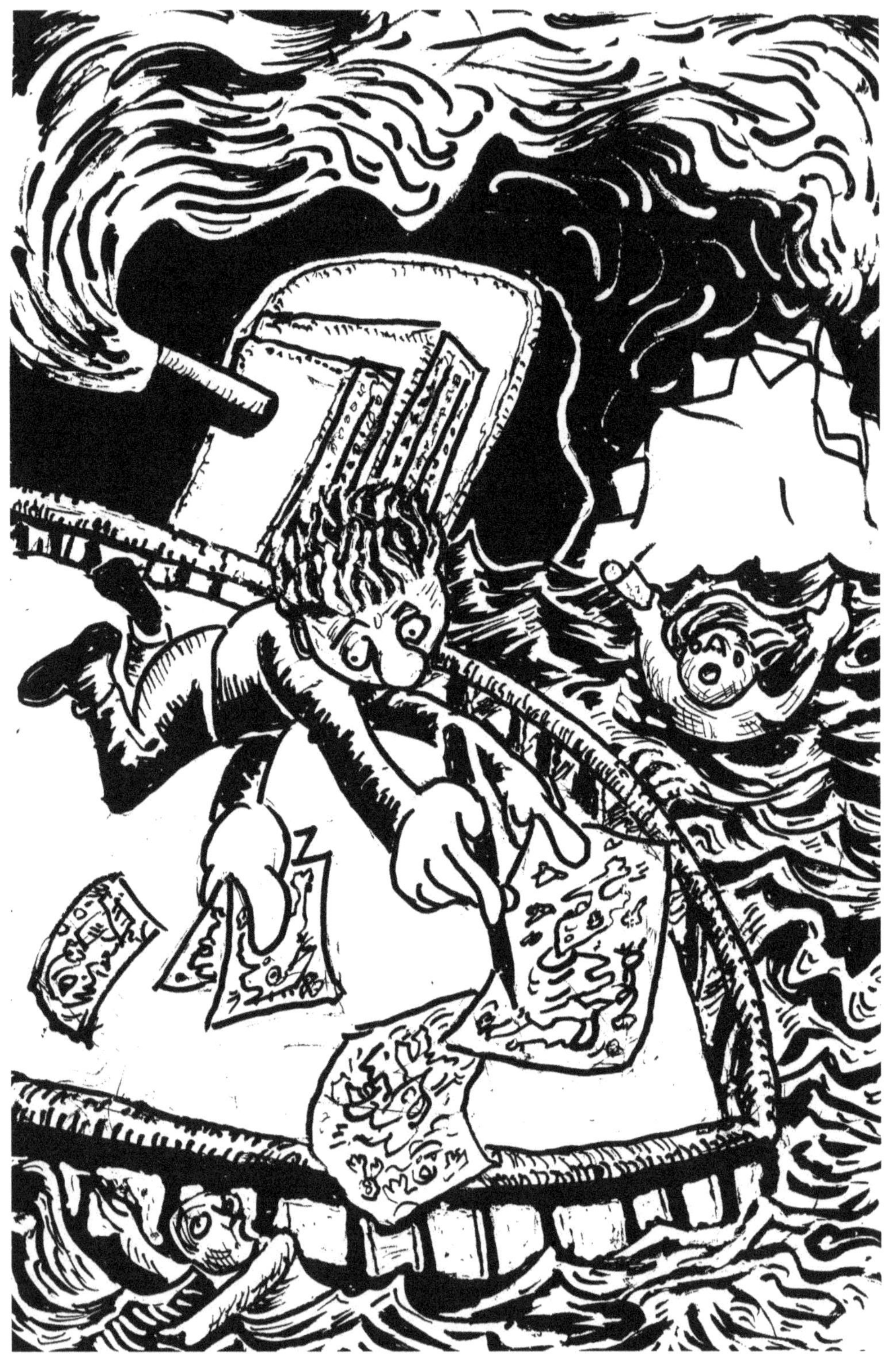

This Is How My Drawings Begin

THIS IS HOW MY DRAWINGS BEGIN.

I have an urge to draw—not necessarily an urge to draw anything in particular. I am like a traveler who loves traveling and doesn't care that much where his journey takes him.

Once I have decided to draw, I select a piece of paper. It has a specific size and shape. Its edges are clearly defined. It's flat. It's usually, but not necessarily white; it has texture and weight. It's the ballpark before the players emerge from their dugouts, the field of battle waiting to receive the blood of the wounded, the bed on which lovers soon will lie.

The emptiness of the page calls out to be filled. It doesn't care how. Nevertheless materials impose limitations. A sheet of paper can be smooth or rough. Marker pens may be new with sharp points or old and stubby. Matter is disobedient. It has a mind of its own. My hand trembles, more so of late as a result of an autoimmune disease which affects my nerves and muscles. My pen may run dry or deposit an unwanted puddle of ink. Every encounter with the material world—wiggling spark plug wires to see why the car won't start, peering under the sink to find the source of a leak—is an encounter with the resistant and unexpected.

Having selected my materials, I am now ready to begin. I shed the concerns that dog my daily life. This moment before I place the first mark on the page is enjoyable in itself. It's a moment to savor.

I make the first mark.

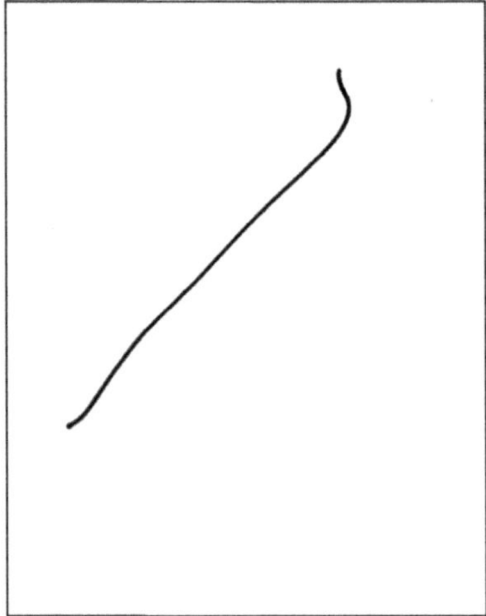

If I'm not trying to represent anything in particular, it's of little concern to me where it's placed on the page. I can close my eyes and begin wherever the pen lands or take a stain or ink blotch that's already there as a starting point. The first mark is exploratory—it's my shout on the edge of a canyon to see if there's an echo.

Within the boundary of the page everything is permitted. I could have made my first mark anywhere, but now it is where it is and nowhere else. A die is cast. The next mark must of necessity relate to the first. Freedom is giving birth to its limits.

As a dog pisses on a lamppost to mark its territory, so now I have begun to mark the space of the page as mine. The line of black ink on the white sheet of paper, unlike any image I may have had in my head, is out there in the space of the world. It is so-and-so many centimeters from the edge of the page. It is oriented in such-and-such a direction. It has length and breadth.

With my first mark, the vast realm of possibility has shrunk precipitously. I am on a path that is not entirely of my own making.

I make my second mark.

I could choose to put it anywhere on the page. But whatever choice I make will be a choice about how one line relates to another. The first line has a gravitational pull on the second.

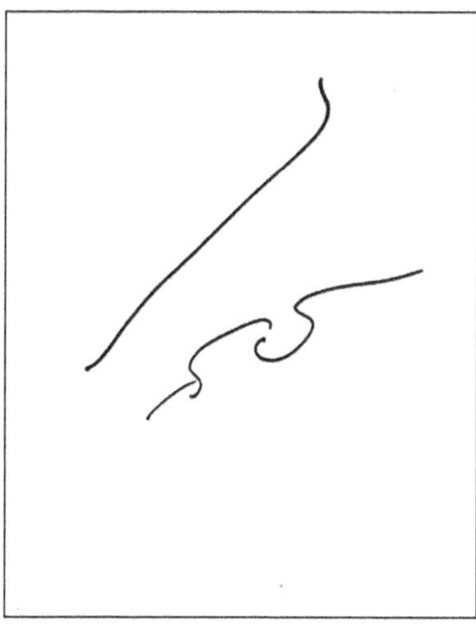

I add more lines and squiggles:

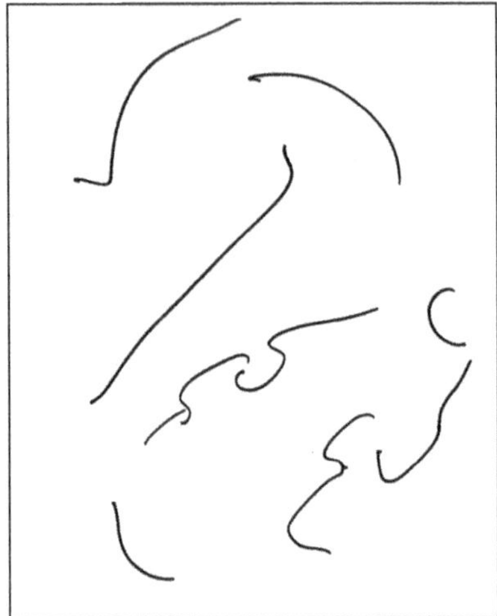

A whole field of relations has now been established. Out of the nothing with which I began a shape is emerging like a spirit that has decided to inhabit a body, like water vapor that is invisible until it condenses into rain when the temperature drops.

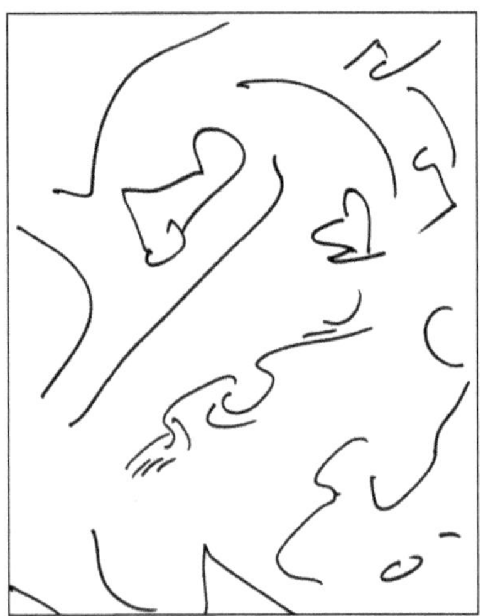

I continue to draw, connecting lines I've already drawn with one another and adding new ones. The lines I have drawn, swiftly without thinking much, betray my state of mind, just as blips in the jiggly line drawn by a polygraph betray the liar.

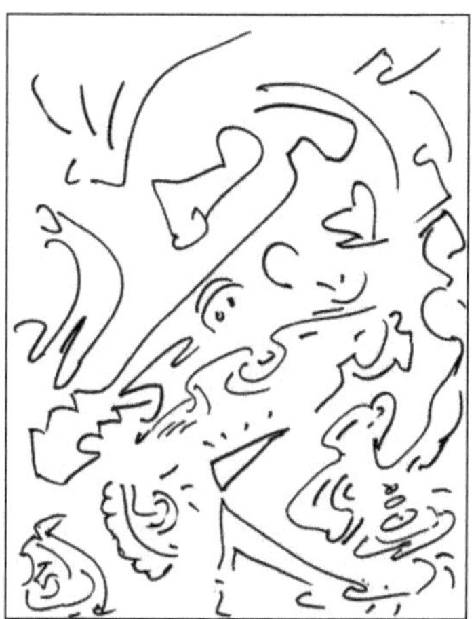

I still do not "see" the finished work. There is no model in my mind that I consult before adding a line here, a squiggle there. Instead there is constant feedback. I look at what I've done. I sense that more is needed, that I'm not *there* yet, wherever there may be.

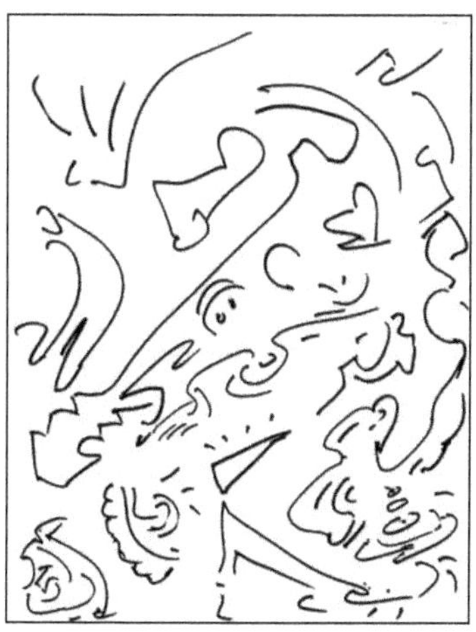

Before I started, the horizon of possibilities I imagined for my work was immense. It included all the art I've ever seen. I might have in mind a Matisse, or a Rivera, or a Benin bronze, or the last drawing I did just before this one. But the horizon shrinks as the work progresses. It quickly becomes clear what the work will *not* be. It won't be a Matisse, or a Rivera, or even that last Osha propped up against a corner of my desk. I still do not know, except in the vaguest way, where I am headed. But I am finding out.

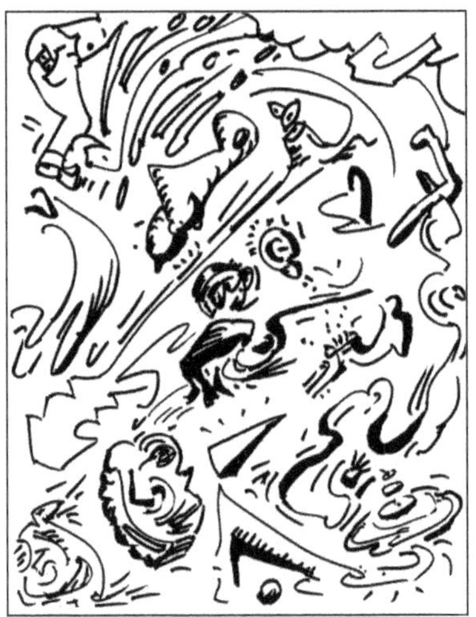

With each new mark more is determined and I have fewer options. The drawing imposes its own necessity. It is no longer the case that any line will do as well as another. The number of available choices diminishes.

The blank page awaiting the first mark, the empty stage awaiting the entrance of the actors, the silence before the music begins represents unlimited possibility within strict boundaries. But the freedom in which anything is possible is sterile unless, in freedom, the artist finds a way to impose limits. As I draw I must make choices, and those choices engender others, and so on until the work is completed. In the finished work, every line and color, every patch of dark and light, every shape and all the spaces between the shapes feel necessary. A hair's breadth off in one direction or another, the slightest change in value or hue, can spell ruin.*

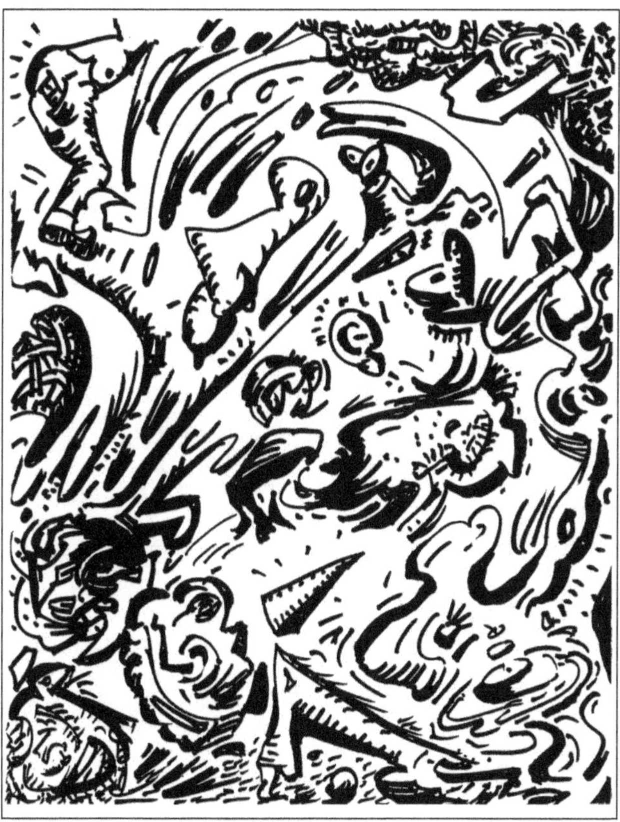

* Well, yes and no. I'm never sure I'm done with a drawing. I think I've got it right, and then I come back the next day and it looks like crap. What seemed necessary one day seems ridiculous the next.

I thicken some lines here, fill in spaces there with curving lines to suggest volume. And then I'm done. This is as far as I will go. For now.

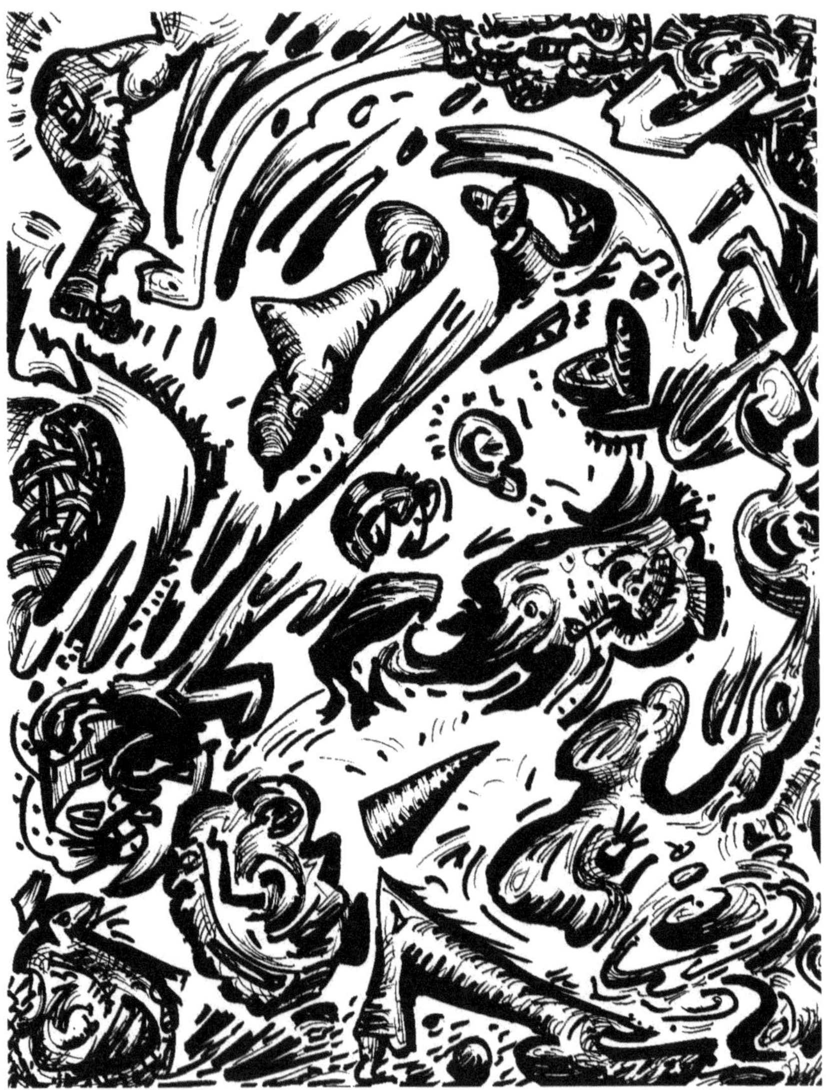

Osha Neumann *Kick Butt* (2010)

Form has emerged from formlessness; freedom has given birth to what I hope is a meaningful necessity. The drawing is an Osha. It's me. And it's not me. It's me in the way a *Still Life with Apples* is a Cézanne or a *Vase with Sunflowers* is a van Gogh. There is no more intimate relationship between a person and an object in the world than that which exists between artists and the art they make. But intimacy can breed indifference. Always a new blank sheet of paper, a newly primed canvas beckons. Artists are serially monogamous with the art they make.

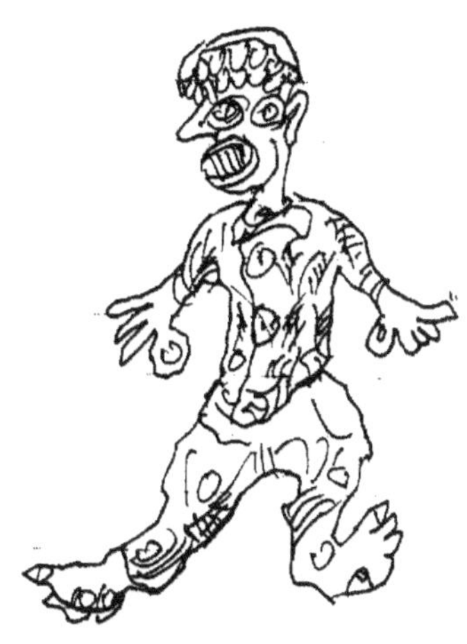

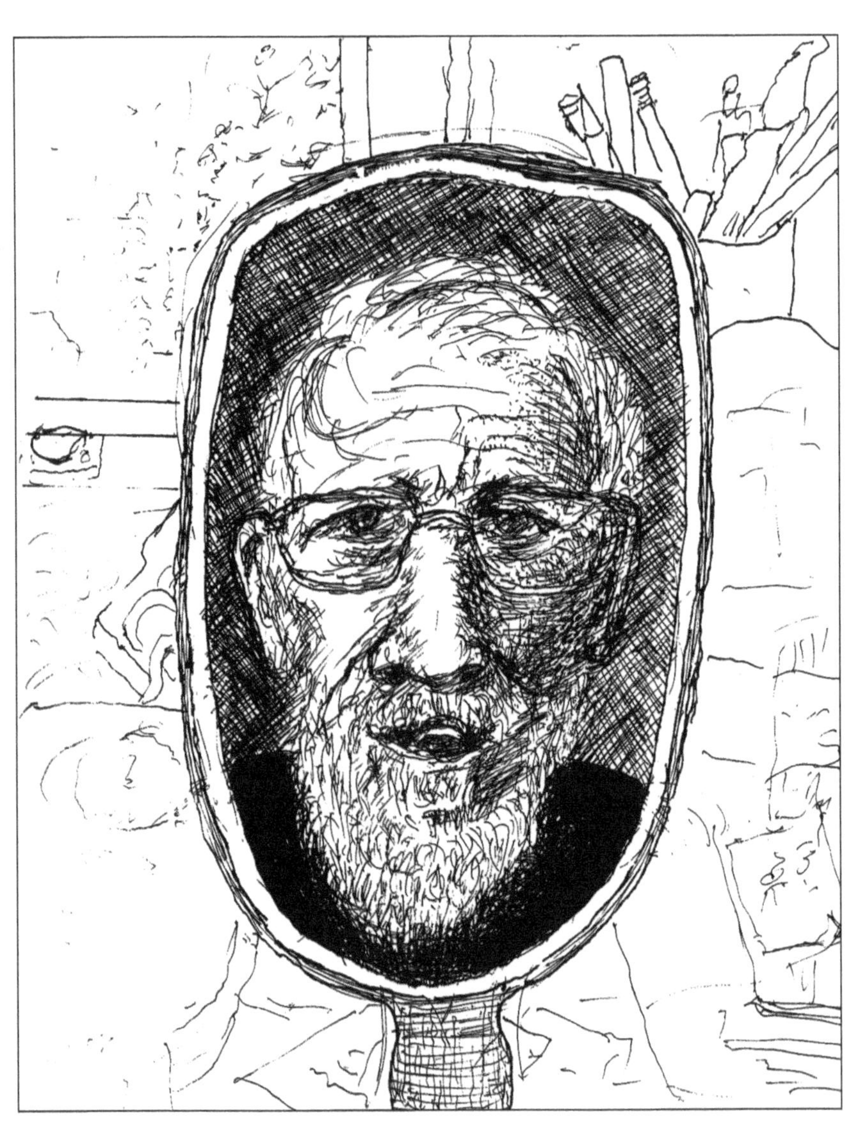

Life Drawing

LIFE DRAWING. IT'S a funny term. It's what in art schools they call drawing from a model. Usually naked. Usually a woman. Drawing still lifes of bottles and fruit—that's not life drawing. Life = naked women.

But let us use the term more broadly to mean drawing the life around us, be it birds, beasts, buildings, or bodies.

The drawing that I made to illustrate "This Is How My Drawings Begin" is not a life drawing. It began without reference to anything *out there.*

How is a life drawing different? They both begin with a blank piece of paper.

But no, the blank piece of paper is not the true beginning. The beginning, more properly, is the intention to make a drawing. And there, at that beginning, the two types of drawing diverge. When I set out to do the drawing that illustrates how my drawings begin, my intention was simply to make a drawing, not to make a drawing *of* something. I let the process take me where it would. To put it another way, I decided *not* to draw from life, *not* to be limited in any way. In the past that choice—to make a drawing without a subject—would have been incomprehensible. Perhaps a sign of madness. These days it's unremarkable.

So now I intend to make a life drawing. I've decided to draw a self-portrait. The blank page makes no demands on me. I could do with it what I like. But I have placed a demand on myself. I have decided what I want to happen in that free space. There will be surprises. Otherwise there would be no point in making the drawing. But the framework within which those surprises occur has been fixed.

Why have I decided to draw myself? For one thing I'm a readily available subject. For another, I find myself interesting. Drawing myself will be a way of taking stock, like checking my blood pressure. It's a way of asking: "How do I relate to myself today? And how do I relate to the image of myself in the mirror?" It is also a way of asking another question: "How will my drawing stack up against all the self-portraits that painters have painted and drawn over the centuries?" By drawing myself, I am placing myself in a lineage of artists who have drawn themselves.

I lean my little hand mirror against a container with pens and pencils and scissors that sits on my desk. The mirror has a handle, which is prevented from slipping by the edge of a pad of paper. The arrangement is precarious. I have to stoop slightly to see myself.

I make my first mark. Or rather cluster of marks.

I can not, as I did in the first drawing, place them just anywhere. They must—because this is the limit I have imposed upon my freedom—conform to something that I see in the mirror. And they must "work" in the finished drawing, considered simply as a drawing. Whether the drawing looks like me or not will matter less in the end than whether it's a good drawing. Burdened with this double duty, I draw tentatively, unsure whether I'm getting it right. By contrast, free of the obligation to represent, I drew the swooshes and squiggles of my first drawing swiftly and cleanly.

When I did the first drawing, my undivided attention was on the piece of paper and the marks I made on it with my pen. Now, from the beginning, my attention is divided. I look up at the mirror, and then down at the page. Up. Down. Up. Down. Only after all those ups and downs do I take the plunge and make my mark. Having made it, I look up again to check the relation between the mark I have made and the face in the mirror staring back at me.

I've decided to start with the top of my head. The curved line that I draw must replicate the curve I see in the mirror. My head is not a billiard ball. I have to draw hair. Already I confront an impossibility. Draw every hair? There's no way. I must find a shorthand.

As I continue to draw, my attention will shuttle back and forth between my image in the mirror and the paper on which I am drawing until the drawing is finished. This is called "sketching." Gradually as I sketch, my face appears on the page, like an image on film in the developing bath of some throwback photographer who has not yet entered the digital age.

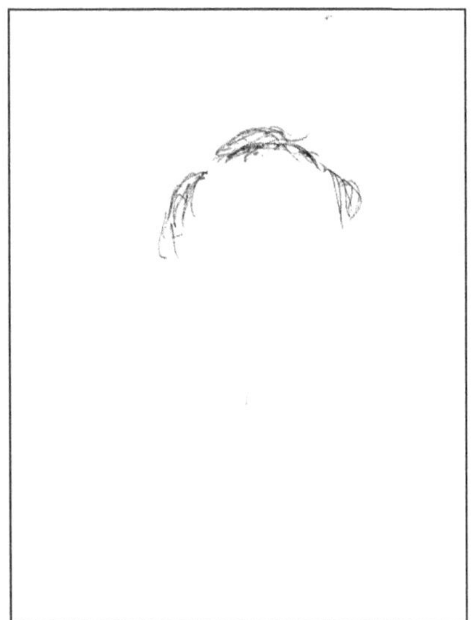

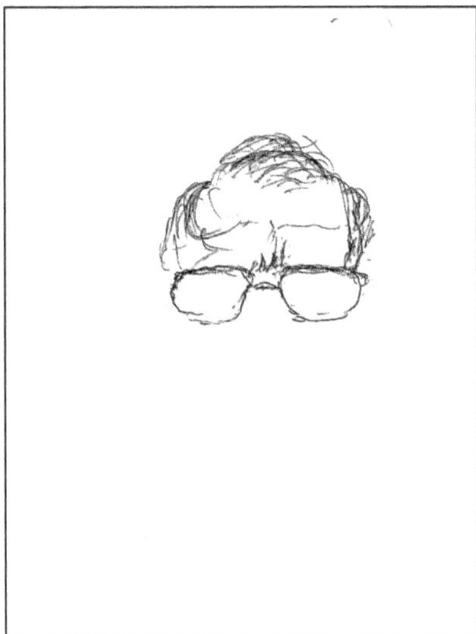

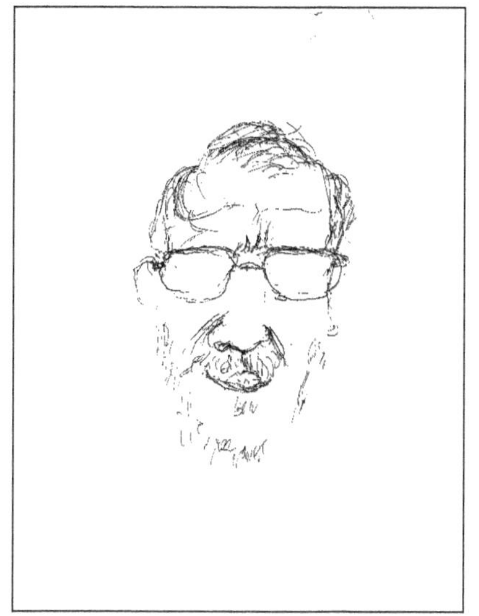

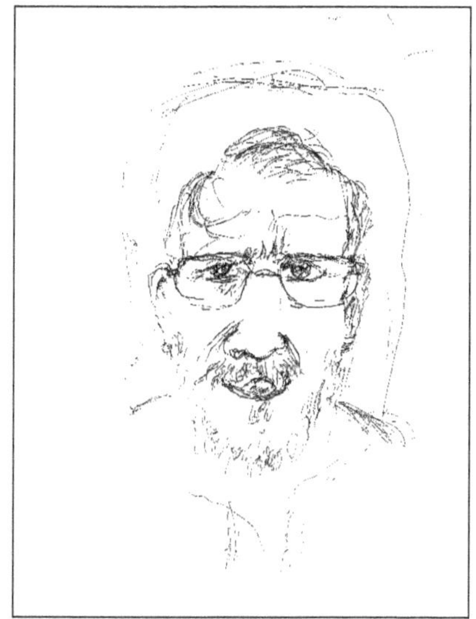

When I concentrate, I tend to stick out my tongue, so I portray myself that way.

I have decided not to invent. I want to see where drawing and reality diverge on their own accord, without my intentionally slipping the reins that hold me to what I see before me. So I need to be careful. The glasses, the nose, the ears, the mouth with my tongue sticking out, have to be shaped correctly and be in correct proportion to each other. The oval outline of my face cannot be too wide or too narrow.

In the beginning, this is all that concerns me. But then new problems arise. I have a white beard. How do I draw a white beard with a black pen? I'm a white man but my skin is not as white as my beard. I notice, however, that where the light falls on my cheekbones, they are lighter than my beard. And my entire face has more light on it than the off-white wall that is reflected behind me in the mirror. How do I convey these relations? The difference between the darkness of shadows and the brightness of sunlight is greater than the difference between white and black. Pigment has nowhere near the range of light. So I'm going to fudge it. Compromises are unavoidable. They may be compromises that are sanctioned by convention, but they are compromises nevertheless.

I begin by crosshatching to represent the shadows on the face.

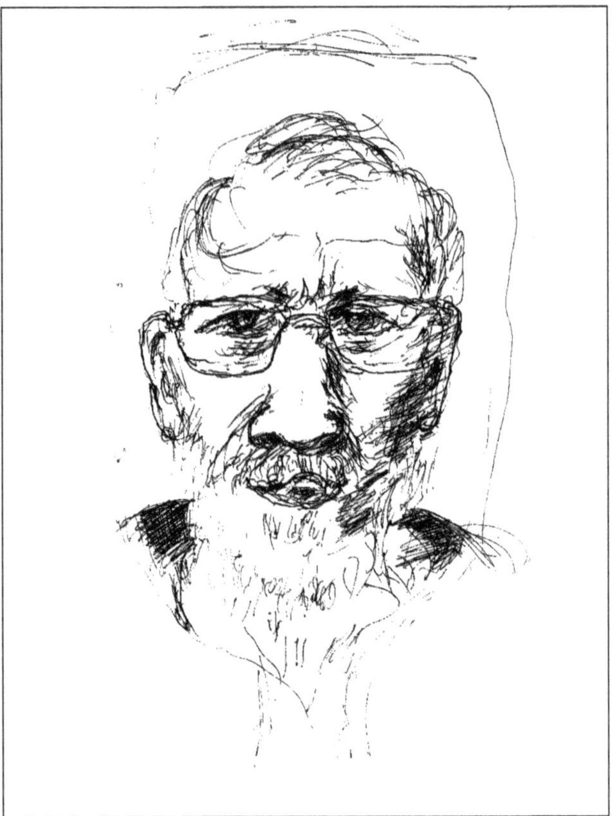

Then I crosshatch around my face to make it stand out from the background.

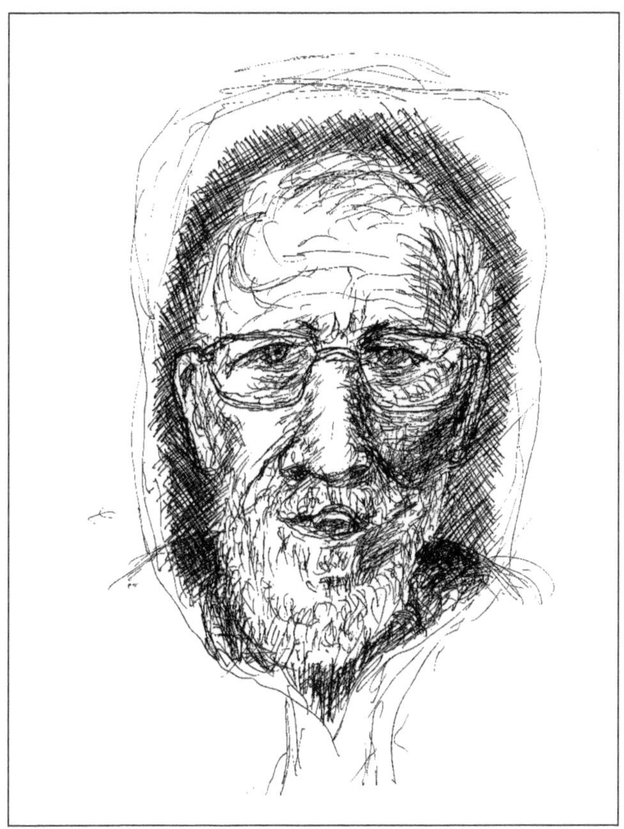

The coat I am wearing is black, blacker than the shadows on my face, but there is no way that I can portray the subtle distinction between the shadowed side of my face and the sunlit side of my jacket. So I don't even try. I make the entire jacket black.

Now that I have more or less got the proportions of the face right and have suggested something of the range of light, shadow, and local color, there remains the problem of composition. There isn't any. The drawing looks incomplete. I had tentatively sketched in the outline of the mirror. Now I firm it up.

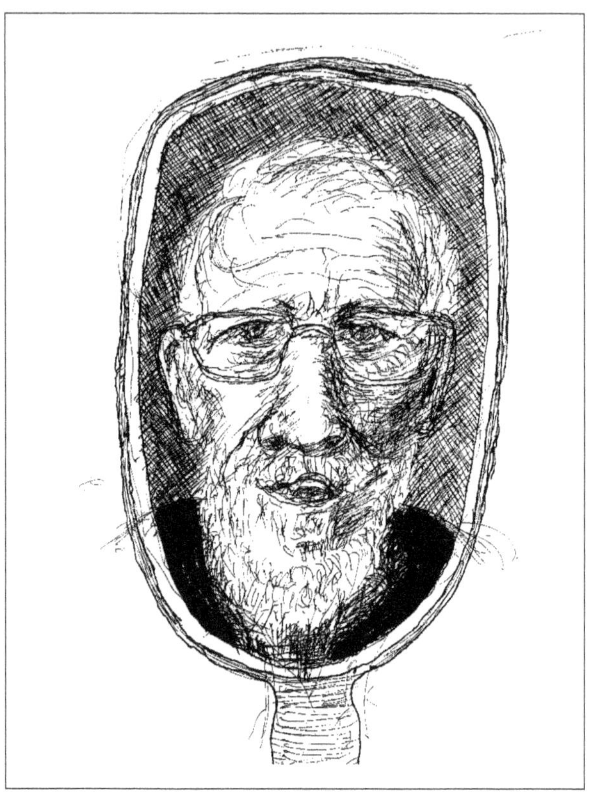

Defining the edges of the mirror does not solve the problem of composition. What do I do with the area outside its frame? Do I draw the clutter on my desk and the window behind it? Do I crosshatch to represent light and dark and the local color of things? I despair of capturing all that complexity. The light outside the window is brighter than anything inside my office, certainly brighter than my reflection in the mirror, but the highest value that I can obtain in my drawing is pure white, and I've already used that for the beard. The representational imperative I've imposed on myself is not strong enough to overcome my resistance to tackling what seem like overwhelming problems. So I give up. I just sketch in the suggestion of a cluttered desk and the window behind and leave it at that.

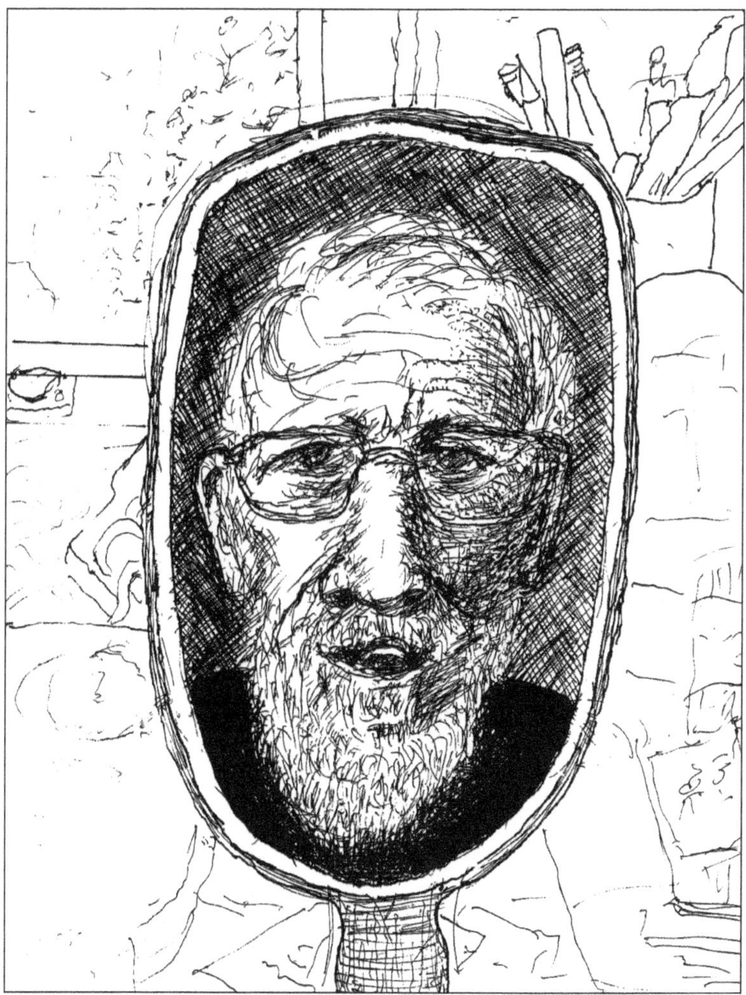

I'm done. It's not my best drawing or my worst. The contrast between the sketchy treatment of the clutter on my desk and the more detailed depiction of the reflection in the mirror suggests two different orders of reality: reality reflected in the mirror, and reality directly encountered, although making a statement about this distinction was not my intention.

I put the drawing away. A few days later, when I look at it again, I like it better. As I was drawing, I was acutely aware that reality was so much richer and more nuanced than my pitiful representation. But now the mirror is no more, I dropped and broke it while returning it to my bedroom. The items on my desk have been rearranged. Time has passed. The drawing remains.

What have I learned trying to draw myself in a mirror? Something about the limits of representation. And perhaps something about the unbredgeable between art and life which all artists confront when they paint from life, artists such as—van Gogh, for example.

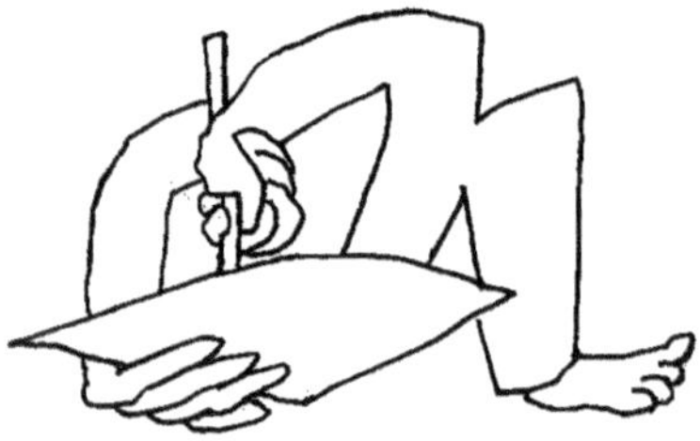

Van Gogh, for Example

Here's another landscape: Setting Sun? Rising Moon?

A summer sun anyway.

Town violet, orb yellow, sky blue-green. The heat contains every possible shade: old gold, copper, green and red gold, yellow gold, yellow bronze, red-green.

Canvas of 30, square.

I painted it with the *mistral* raging, my easel fixed to the ground with iron stakes, a trick I recommend to you. One sticks the legs of the easel firmly into the ground, then by their side one drives in an iron stake about 2 ft. long; then one binds then all together with cords. Like that you can work in the wind.

Vincent van Gogh, Letter to Emile Bernard, about June 20, 1888[2]

EARLY IN THE morning on the last day of spring, van Gogh sets out from his little room in Arles to paint a picture. The *mistral,* a cold, dry northerly wind, is blowing. He carries an easel and when he finds a place he likes he stakes it to the ground.

Van Gogh places his canvas on the easel. Like the pieces of paper on which I did my drawings, his canvas is a plain white rectangle. When I did my life drawing, I knew before I began that I wanted to draw a self-portrait. Van Gogh, as he walks out into the fields, has formed the intention of painting a landscape.

Once he has staked his easel to the ground and the canvas is in place, Van Gogh looks around. Over there, perhaps a mile away, is the town.

Between the town and where he stands are wheat fields, the stalks of wheat bending in the wind. Looking down, van Gogh can see his feet, shod in clumsy peasant boots. A foot or so in front of him is the easel holding the canvas. The distances—town to boots to easel—are all easily measurable. But where in this picture is van Gogh, where is his *seeing*, his self-consciousness and consciousness of the world around him? Where is his "I"? It's neither here nor there. His "I" is nowhere.

Van Gogh has adjusted the easel to its proper height. He has arranged his paints and brushes on the narrow shelf beneath the bar on which his canvas rests. The attention he paid to these preliminaries has a quite different quality from the attention he now turns to the landscape he is about to paint. All the business of life, of which the adjustment of the easel was a part, is set aside. In turning away from the world of business, he turns toward himself and toward the world in a new way. He sees the town in the distance. He is aware of his seeing and of what it is that he sees. These awarenesses are not separate and distinct and they are not the same. They merge and they do not merge.

Arles is in the distance. He is going to paint a view of it. The town is not van Gogh. It's over there. And van Gogh is not the town. He's here. His boots are planted on the earth, a mile from its roofs and steeples. But is it that simple? All there is of the town, *for van Gogh,* is the seeing of it. The *sight* of the town is not "over there." Nor is it "in his head." The idea that consciousness is "in" the space of our head is the result of falsely equating consciousness with the gray matter of our brain. Consciousness is not in space the way gray matter is, or boots, or easels. It's neither here nor there. Or perhaps, more accurately, it's both here and there insofar as there is a "here" and "there."*

* Yes, I know. I have stumbled, no, strode purposefully, into the La Brea tar pit of philosophy—the mind/body problem where god knows how many previous explorers have found themselves inextricably stuck in a quagmire of unanswerable questions. Perhaps those questions are unanswerable because our logic has no room for contradiction. Or perhaps they are unanswerable because, like the questions that arise when we think deeply about art, they lead us to a place beyond reach of language.

Van Gogh is the town. And he is not. The "not-van Goghness" of the town constitutes a break in the heart of being, van Gogh's being and the being of the world. It isolates him. It leaves him with a wound that closes only when he paints.*

We say "I." We think "I." That inescapable columnar capital stands at the center of all language and thought. It holds up the entire edifice. But it's structurally unsound. It stands soldier straight, like a West Point cadet, concealing the fault line that runs between the observing the self and the self that is observed. Some of us are able to hold ourselves together despite that fault. At what cost? Others, like van Gogh, repeatedly break down under the effort.

The "I" can maintain its precarious integrity only in relation to a world from which it is and is not separate. We are born into this contradiction and live it as an incompleteness, as a project, until we die. Separation and self-consciousness are born together and die together.

When the boundary between the self and the world is obliterated—in extreme pain, alcoholic stupor, ecstasy, and orgasm, when we fall toward sleep and death approaches—the world is lost to us and we to it. The observer-self and self that is observed merge and in that merger the "I" approaches its extinction. Death is the ultimate resolution of all contradiction. When pain ceases, the alcohol wears off, the moment of ecstasy passes, and orgasm works its way to climax, when we rouse ourselves from sleep, and death decides to wait a few more days, and then the "I" re-forms and with the reconstitution of the "I" returns also—distance, otherness,

* What is "being" that there can be a break in its heart? I image a crack, as in the earth, a chasm, but it is a chasm neither in space nor in time, a chasm in being that might as well be chasm in nothingness. "Being" is not an "it"; There are no predicates we can ascribe to being. In English "being" is a participle, a noun made from verb. Therefore we are forced by the English language to think of it as a "something," which it clearly isn't. In German it is not an "it." It is an infinitive, a verb without tense, the root of all predicates by which we ascribe existence to things. Philosophers since the Greeks have struggled with the concept and I, who am no philosopher, toss it around like a kid playing with a wiffle ball. I am not unmindful of the seriousness of the game. I speak, reluctantly, of a space opening up in being, a falling apart, because that is best I can do in my gesturing toward the ineffable, and yes, "gesturing toward the ineffable," is exactly what I accused all those grandiloquent art critics of doing.

perspective, the hardness of the rock, the shadows on the hillside, the river thrashing hungrily in its bed.

We spend our days searching for a lost unity: for healing love, for a landscape we can lie down in, for a song that carries us away. The "I" longs for the end of its isolation. In art and love we taste its possibility. But always, inevitably, love and art return us to a world of distances. The longing for oneness and for unity can never be fulfilled in life, because, if it were, the "I" would cease to exist. The wholeness we long for can only be achieved at the cost of life itself. Death seeking, life seeking, we rush pell-mell through our lives, pausing now and then for a song and a glimpse of beauty.

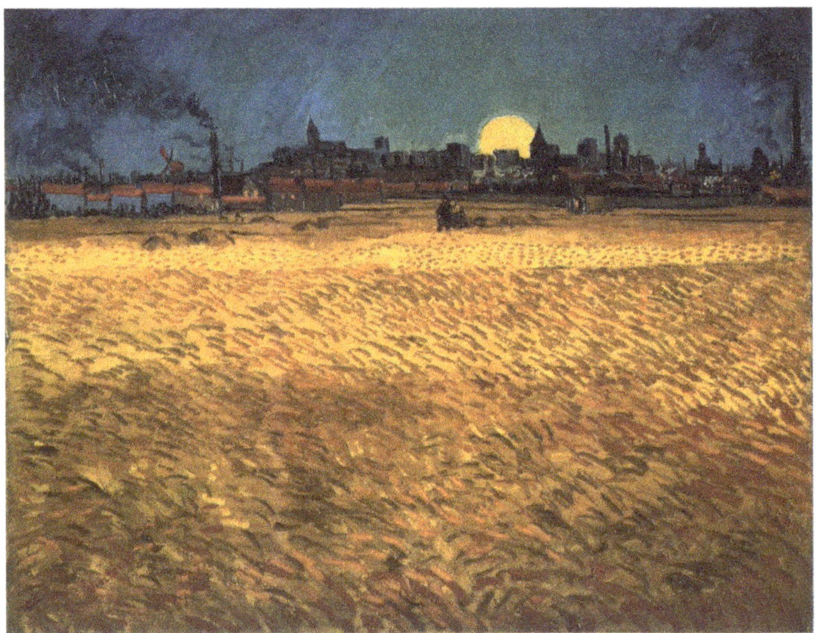

Van Gogh, *The Summer Evening (View of Arles at Sunset)*, 1888

Let us return to van Gogh, still painting in the wheat field. A yellow sun is descending toward the horizon. Purple shadows lengthen. He squeezes richly odorous oil paints out of their tubes and smears them on his pallet. He stabs his brush into the mounds of purple, blue, orange, and yellow and applies them to the canvas. Each of his brushstrokes is van Gogh, each is, depending on where he directs his brush, town or wheat or sun. The canvas becomes a world. But unlike the world he must inhabit until his death, the world of the canvas is not split. His "I" is not *over here*; the "not-I," *over there*. Within the frame of the canvas, I and not-I are fused in an impossible unity.

Van Gogh puts down his brush. He is simultaneously exhausted and exhilarated. He walks away from the easel and examines his painting. Is it finished? No, not quite. It wants a little more purple here, a few more brush strokes there. He picks up his brush, adds purple in a shadow and a flurry of brush strokes that become wheat in the wheat field. He steps away again. The light is changing rapidly. It's time to go. He packs up his easel and takes the painting home to his little, sparsely furnished bedroom. Meanwhile the sun sets; shadows fall across the fields. And then it's night—and then it's day again. Van Gogh resumes his wonderful and unbearable existence.

Nothing has changed. The gulf that lies within himself, and the gulf between himself and the world has not diminished. His bed with the red coverlet, his two straight back wooden chairs with wicker seats, the little wooden table next to his bed, the bowl and basin that rest on it, the mirror on the wall—all exist apart from him, across a great divide. A chasm within being yawns when he wakes up in the morning, accompanies him throughout his day, and closes only when he falls asleep at night. He must paint again as the serial killer must kill again, as the lover must embrace again, as the revolutionary must return again and again to the barricades. *La Lucha Continua.*

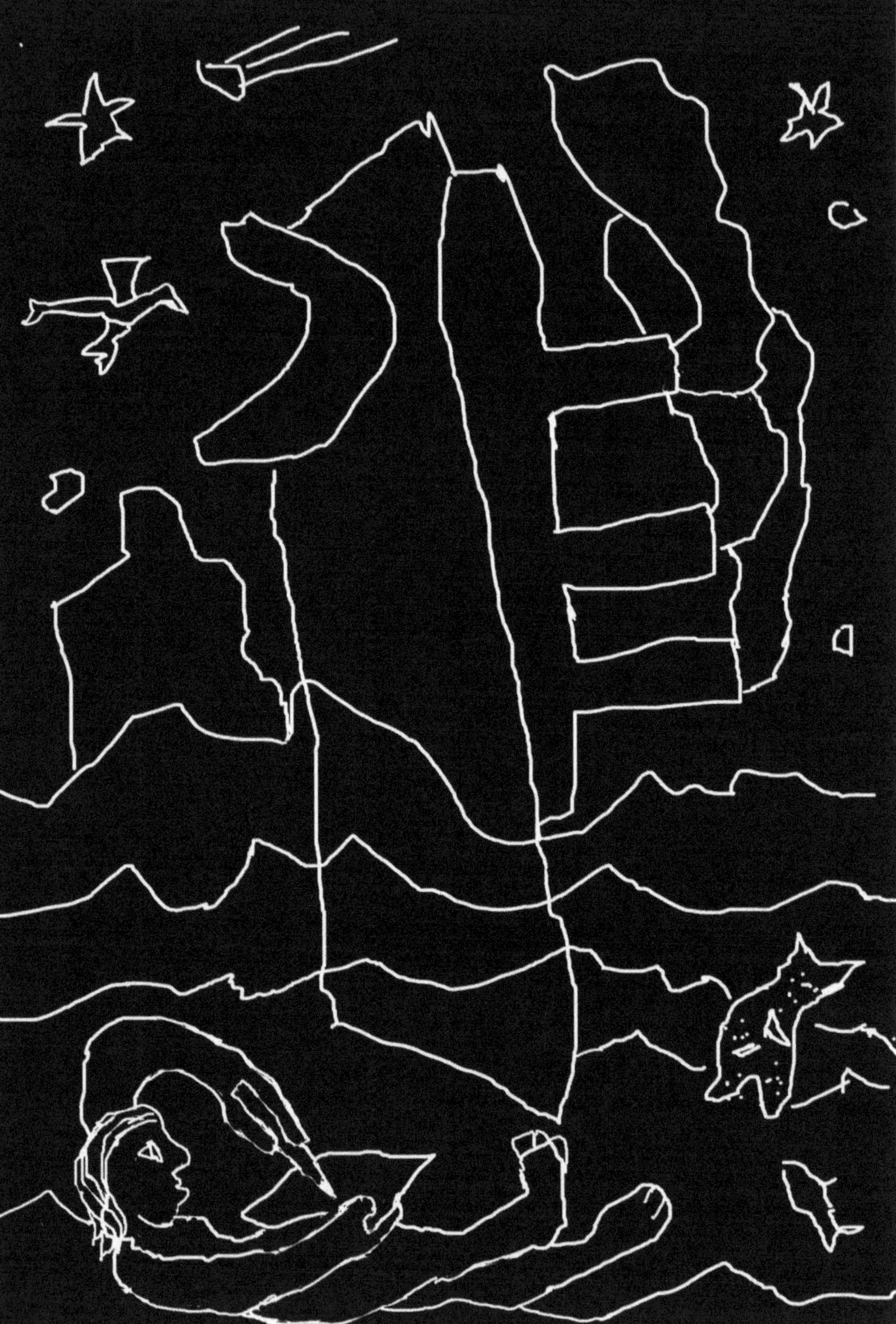

Failure of Representation, Redemption by Beauty

VAN GOGH WRITES to Emile Bernard, regarding *The Summer Evening*:

> Sometimes I work terribly fast. Is that a fault? I can't help it.
>
> The large canvas of 30, for example, *The Summer Evening* was painted at one sitting.
>
> I can't work on it again: shall I destroy it? Why should I? I went out specially to do it while the *mistral* was raging.
>
> It's more the intensity of thought than the tranquility of touch we are after: but in circumstances such as these where one is driven to work impulsively, on the spot and directly from nature, I doubt whether it is always possible to preserve a calm well-ordered touch. After all it's rather like suddenly being assaulted with a rapier.
>
> Vincent van Gogh, Letter to Emile Bernard, last week of June 1888.[3]

A rapier? A rapier stabs and penetrates. Our life drains out through the wound. The storm? It's an enveloping force. It shakes the wheat, shakes the easel, shakes the painting on the easel. And the artist? It shakes him too. Within and without, the storm rages. What is it that he struggles to capture in the painting? Surely the world as appearance: setting sun, wheat fields, Arles in the distance, vibrating light, movement and color. But what else? He tells Bernard: "It's more the intensity of thought than the tranquility of touch we are after." The outer storm is, to use the term popularized by T. S. Eliot, the "objective correlative" of an inner intensity.*

"Show don't tell," is the mantra instilled in would-be writers. Eliot's dictum that the only way of expressing emotion in art is through an "objective correlative" implies that the object, which stands for the emotion, is separate from the emotion it evokes. But it is precisely the independence of the object from the emotion that disappears when van Gogh paints outside in a storm. The storm without and the storm within are both in every brushstroke. And even when there is no storm, van Gogh paints as if a mistral's raging.** His "intensity of thought" roils the starry night, sunflowers in a vase, the beard of the postman. To match his inner storm, all the prurient decorum and inhibitions of the natural world must be stripped away. He frees the yellows that lie within the mottled dun of the wheat field and the bright purples that hide in the shadows.

> One starts with a hopeless struggle to follow nature, and everything goes wrong; one ends by calmly creating from one's palate, and nature agrees with it and follows.
>
> Van Gogh, letter to Theo, late October 1885[4]

---

* The only way of expressing emotion in the form of art is by finding an "objective correlative"; in other words, a set of objects, a situation, a chain of events which shall be the formula of that particular emotion; such that when the external facts, which must terminate in sensory experience, are given, the emotion is immediately evoked.

T. S. Eliot "Hamlet and His Problems" in *The Sacred Wood: Essays on Poetry and Criticism*. New York: Alfred A. Knopf, 1921; Bartleby.com, 1996. www.bartleby.com/200/sw9.html [accessed January 8, 2014]

** Sartre captures better than Eliot the relation of object to emotion when he writes of Tintoretto:

> [He] did not choose that yellow rift in the sky above Golgotha to *signify* anguish or to *provoke* it. It is anguish and yellow sky at the same time. Not sky of anguish or anguish sky; it is an anguish become the thing, an anguish which has turned into yellow rift of sky, and which thereby is submerged and impasted by the proper qualities of things, by their impermeability, their extension, their blind permanence, and externality and that infinity of relations which they maintain with other things.

Jean Paul Sartre, *What Is Literature?* Trans. Bernard Frechtman. New York: Philosophical Library, 1949, 9-10.

Art will always be a poor imitation of life. Better than life, perhaps; more lifelike than life itself, but still a poor facsimile. Look over the shoulder of a painter—it could be van Gogh or any lesser artist—as he sits in the *plein-air* before his easel. All around are sky, clouds, fields, trees, sunlight, and shadow. Immediately you become aware of a terrible mismatch. A painting can never capture the immensity of nature, nor its restless incandescence. The landscape is boundless, the canvas a puny rectangle. Countless stalks of wheat make up a wheat field. No painter can paint every stalk—not van Gogh, not even Andrew Wyeth at his most meticulous. Certainly not Osha, defeated in his attempt to draw the clutter on his desk.

Van Gogh paints at one of those turning points in the history of art at which the entire project of representation is called into question. He writes to Bernard, "I devour nature ceaselessly,"[5] and tells his brother Theo that his "great longing is to make those very incorrectnesses, those deviations, remodelings, changes in reality, so that they may become, yes, lies if you like—but truer than the literal truth."[6] He still strives to corral the infinite immensity of appearances, but finds that the "true" colors of the world become lies when transferred onto the canvas and the bright yellows and purples that convey the "intensity of thought" are closer to the truth.

As a faithful reflection of what we see, every painting will be a failure. The path of the painting and the path of the world inevitably diverge. The paradox of realism is that if art were perfectly realistic, it would cease to be art. Even art that is fervently devoted to mirroring appearances transmutes the world of appearance into something other than itself. A mirror is not a work of art, and art is not a mirror. Painting as representation is as much rebellion against the given as submission to its dictates.

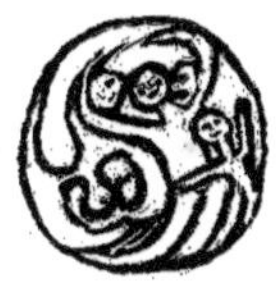

A painting is a world within the world. But unlike the world outside the frame, the painting is bounded and contains nothing that is unintended. Within its borders all that is random and meaningless succumbs to an all-encompassing order.

Experience is boundless. It has no edge. We walk through the world, turning our attention here and there, and find ourselves surrounded by stuff we recognize and can name: my car over there in the parking lot; Joe across the street; the phone on my desk whose ringing now interrupts me. But surrounding the zone of our attention is the penumbra of what is seen without being seen, and what is known without being known. As I walk home from my office, a sort of V-shape appears within the branches of a tree, which disappears when I take another step. I happen to notice it, but if I noticed all the shapes appearing and disappearing I would be lost in a soup of sensation. That V-shape has no meaning or purpose. Meaningless, purposeless, contingent and ever-changing relations of forms and shapes in space characterize the world that we inhabit and are the sign and symptom of its unforgiving otherness.

The sign of the overcoming of that otherness in a work of art is the emergence of a necessity of forms. As the empty space within the margins of the canvas fills with shapes and colors, as areas of dark and light are established, what was arbitrary and contingent in the beginning becomes necessary and essential. The drawing with which I illustrated how my drawings begin was not a drawing of anything in particular. I was under no obligation, as I was when I did the self-portrait, to match shapes on the page to the shapes of anything in the world outside its borders. My line was free to wander where it would. And still, in the end, my freedom was gently but firmly curtailed by the drawing itself.

When a painting depicts something *out there* beyond the edge of the canvas—be it a face in a mirror, a bowl of fruit, or a landscape—the necessity that emerges in the course of the painting is imposed upon the world. A painter working with a model will carefully adjust her position before he begins. Once he starts, she won't be allowed to move a muscle. The angle at which her leg bends, the space that's visible between the crook of her arm and the edge of her torso become crucial elements in the composition. Before she came to work, when she rose from her bed in the morning, got dressed, brushed her teeth, and walked out of her apartment, her body carved shapes in space to which neither she nor anyone else paid any attention. But now is different. In the painting, form that was fleeting and contingent has become the vehicle of meaning.

The contingency of appearances is transformed in the work of art into a necessity of forms. Every line, color, and shape must "work" in relation to every other.* Even the quick sketch by a great artist can be felt as complete in itself. There can be harmony in the most dissonant work, completeness in the most fragmentary.

The necessity which develops in the work of art is not like a law of nature. It can't be proved experimentally; it can't be achieved by following a set of rules. But it is not purely subjective. It is self-evident to those who are moved by works of art and can't be demonstrated to those who aren't. It is discovered in the course of the making of the work and rediscovered in its appreciation. Lines and colors really do require each other. Their need is our need.

Outside the frame of the canvas, objects do not share our needs. The river follows a course of its own devising. If its rapids drown us, we don't expect apologies. But in the painting the colors and lines and shapes that *are* the river fulfill a need that is theirs and also ours. Our need is the object's need and vice versa. Our necessity is its necessity.

The necessity of forms is not purely subjective, just as beauty is not simply in the eye of the beholder. We cannot tell whether we like a flavor

* "It works," or "it doesn't work," is what artists tend to say when critiquing each other's paintings. Art teachers hate the term. They would like something more specific and substantive. But because there are no rules for making a good painting, and because the objective necessity of a line or color can only be discovered by experiencing the painting itself, in the end "it works" is about the best non-explanation we can give for a judgment of aesthetic value, clichéd as it may be.

of ice cream without tasting it. Likewise we can not tell whether a work of art is beautiful without experiencing its beauty. Nevertheless, beauty is not simply a matter of taste. A great work of art *is* beautiful. Few people would argue that cherry vanilla is objectively better than rocky road. Taste buds differ. But we perceive beauty as a property of the work of art, not of our perceiving.* Across expanses of time and a diversity of cultures, people have joined in awe at Michelangelo's muscular saints, Hokusai's serene Mount Fuji, and the stampeding bison of Lascaux.**

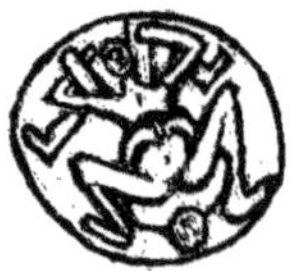

In great works of art, lived experience—contingent, formless, and without boundaries—is re-presented as necessary, whole, and self-contained. Time is defeated. The subjects of all the great paintings of the world wither away but remain fresh on the canvas. Beauty grants a reprieve to the fleeting moment that time decrees must die at birth. The dancer posing for Degas develops a cramp and moves her arm, but in his pastel time stands still, her arm curves eternally.

As artistic form comes into being in a space apart from the space of ordinary doing, so it exists in its own time, apart from the time of our

---

* Kant again:

> It would be ridiculous if someone who prided himself on his taste tried to justify [it] by saying: This object (the building you're looking at, the garment that man is wearing, the concert we are listening to, the poem put up to be judged) is beautiful *for me*. For he must not call it *beautiful* if he means only that *he* likes it. Many things may be charming and agreeable to him; no one cares about that. But if he proclaims something to be beautiful, then he requires the same liking from others; he then judges not just for himself but for everyone, and speaks of beauty as if it were a property of things.

Immanuel Kant, *Critique of Judgment,* trans. Werner Pluhar (Indianapolis, Hackett Publishing, 1987 § 7, 55-56.) Kant goes on to admit that "This universality requires a major effort . . . to discover its origin." (*Ibid.* § 8, 57) everyday comings and goings. We feel the stillness of the infinite in the serenely smiling Khmer Buddhas of Cambodia. But that stillness is also there in Monet's water lilies, which have no substance apart from the light of the fleeting moment. Van Gogh, in a letter written four days before his death, thanks his brother Theo for his help in producing "some canvases, which even in the cataclysm retain their calm."[7]

Art gives us a world that is complete in itself. It has no need for change. Even ugliness is transformed. The cruelty Goya depicted in his *Disasters of War* cries out for condemnation. It must not continue, even for a moment. And yet in his etchings it lives forever, but no longer victorious. Harmony prevails, but it is an unforgiving harmony within which ugliness, torture, and obscenity retain their appalling power.

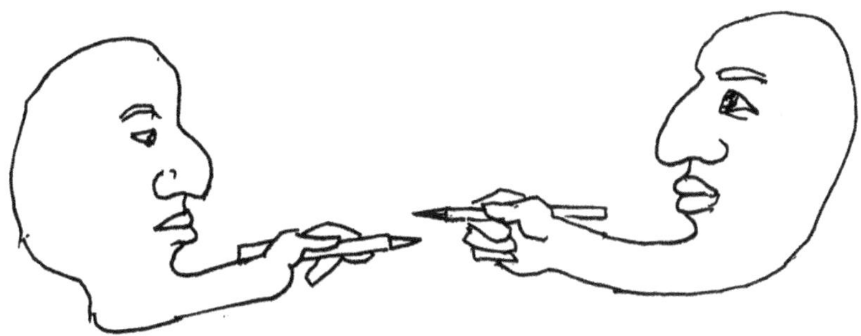

** Of course, this consensus may fluctuate, sometimes wildly over time. Works of art that challenge prevailing conventions often receive a hostile reception. The first group exhibition of Impressionists was greeted with derision and ridicule, as a "laughable collection of absurdities." A joke went around that the "painters' method consists in loading a pistol with several tubes of paint and firing at a canvas, then finishing off the work with a signature." (The wits were ahead of their time. What fun they would've had with Jackson Pollock.)Now the tables are turned. The labored neoclassical productions of the Académie des Beaux-Arts strike us as trite, clichéd and sentimental. There are works of art that I appreciated at one point in my life that I couldn't care less about now. Nevertheless, when I do come across a work of art that excites me, I feel I have made a real discovery which can and should be shared with others.

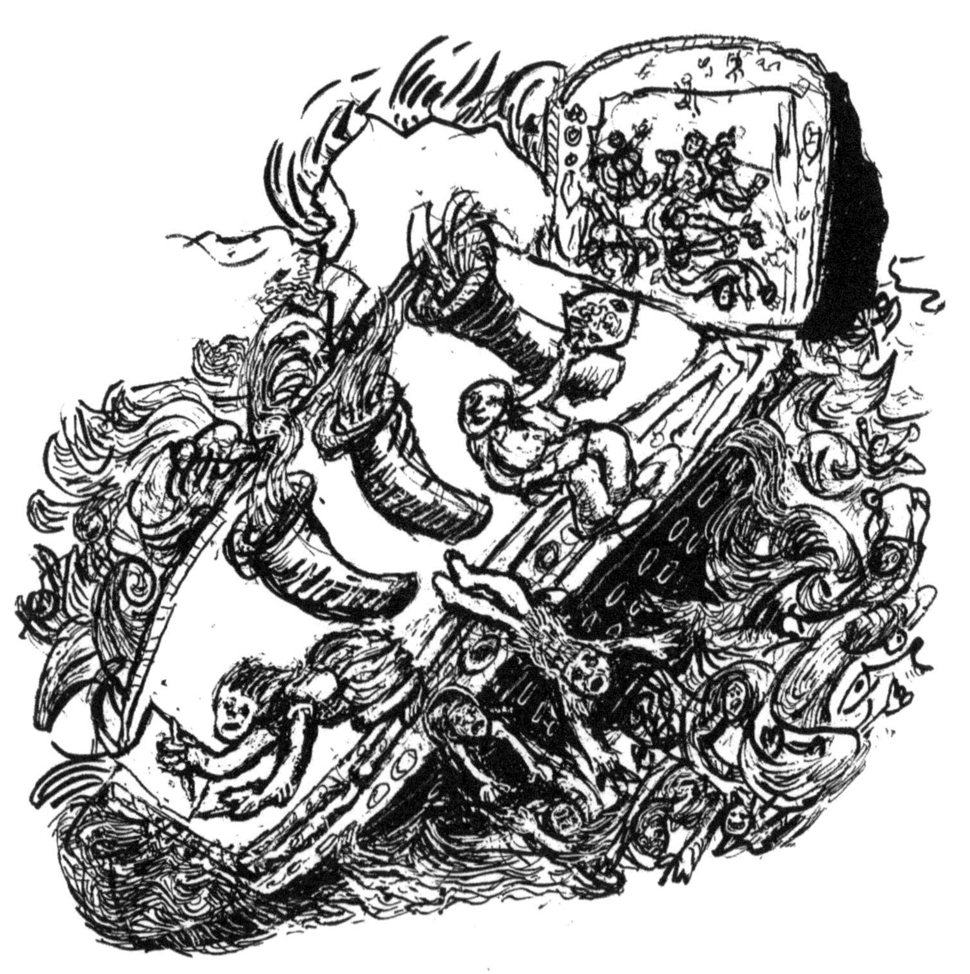

Form Is Content, Content Is Form. Or Is It?

WILLEM DE KOONING and Leonardo da Vinci both painted women, but it would be odd to say the women depicted are the *content* of their paintings. The paintings do not *contain* women as cans of tomatoes contain tomatoes.

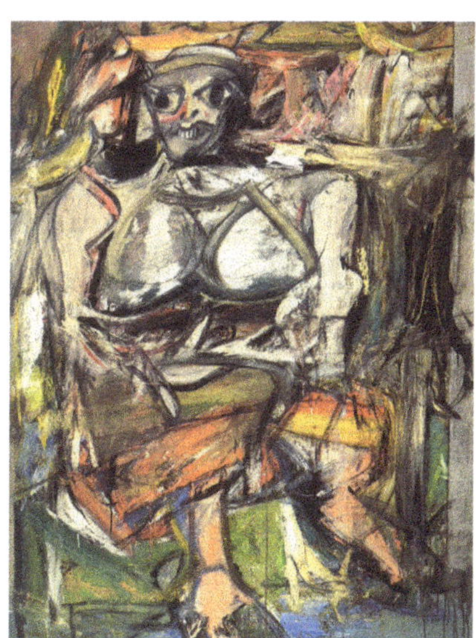

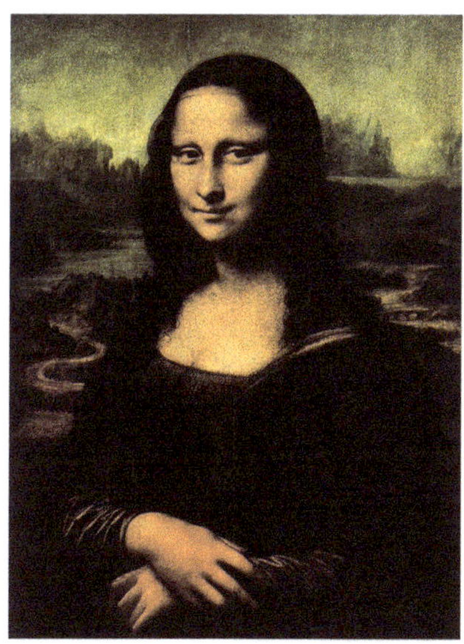

The paintings do not *contain* women, but they are both paintings *of* women. They're not paintings of paint. "What did the artist paint?" is a different question from "How did he paint it?" *How* and *what* may not be separable, but they are distinguishable. There is no form without content, no content without form; inseparable, they nevertheless remain separate; their marriage is never free from the risk that one or the other will be unfaithful.

There are no purely abstract paintings. Elimination of subject matter from a painting is not a distillation process that removes all trace of the color and taste of life. Lines, shapes, and colors are not abstractions. They are what they are, unique and individual. But like all things we encounter in the world they are not orphans. A shape has a kinship with all things similarly shaped, a patch of color with all things similarly colored. Therefore colors and shapes have resonances. And because they are the products of a human hand, guided by a human consciousness, they speak to us of their creator.

We can read in a line drawn on a sheet of paper the state of mind of the artist who drew it. To draw these lines I must relax:

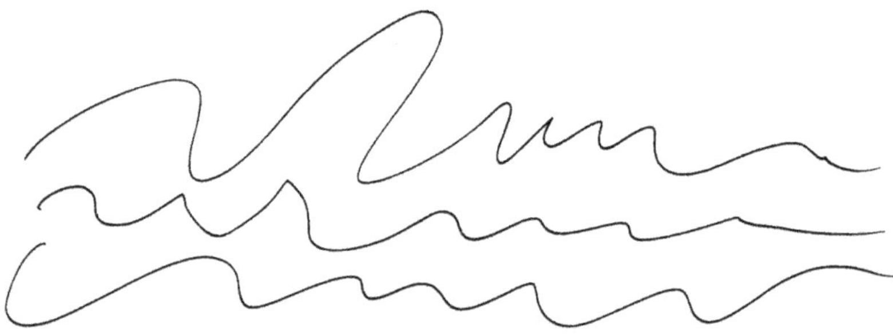

They can't be drawn any other way.

To draw these lines I tighten up:

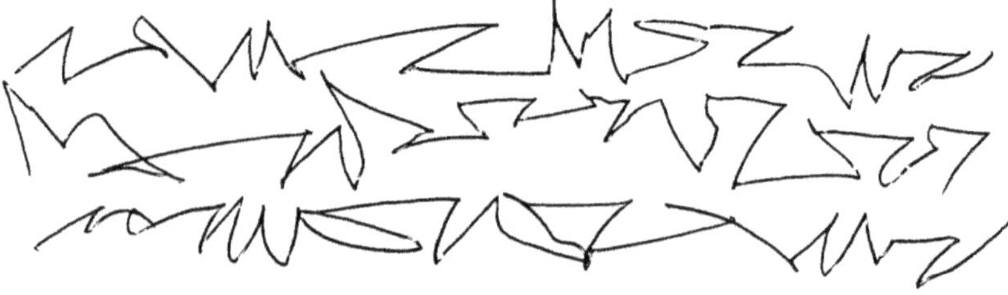

A jagged line requires me to be jagged.

Our response to forms is filled with memories of our encounters with the sharpness of mountain peaks, the soft necks of lovers, the verticality of trees, the horizontality of horizons. A vertical line bisecting a horizontal one:

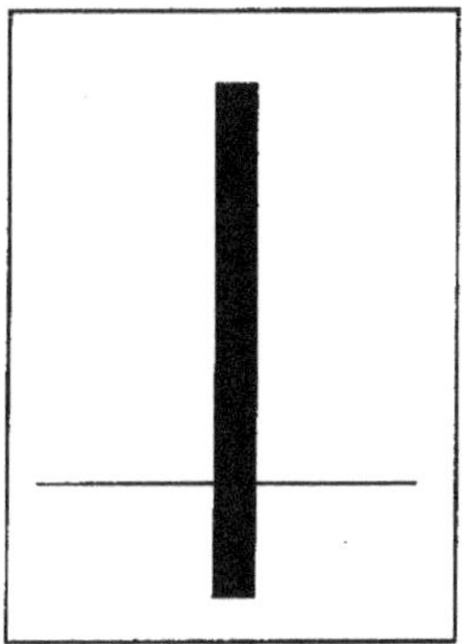

speaks to us the language we learned in a lifetime of treading upon the earth and encountering all that rises from that universal foundation.

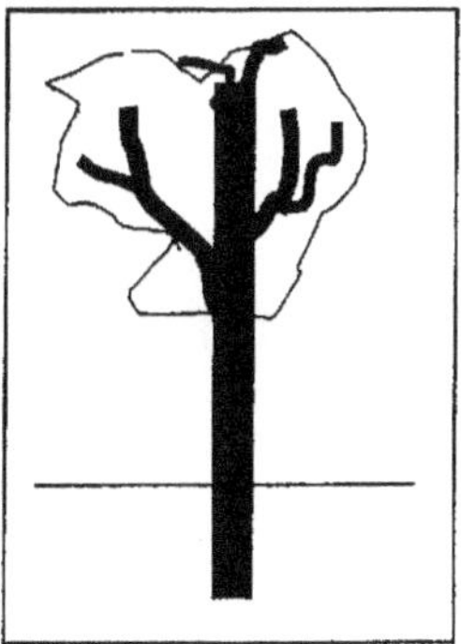

Our response to the color green is informed by our encounters with all of nature's greenery. The bright white of the paper and the blackness of ink speak to us in a language we learned from sunlight and shadow, night and day.

Forms speak the language of our entire experience. And sometimes, in addition, they represent. This vertical—hand drawn to give it some character—says: "I may stand alone in the white space, but I am of the family of all things vertical."

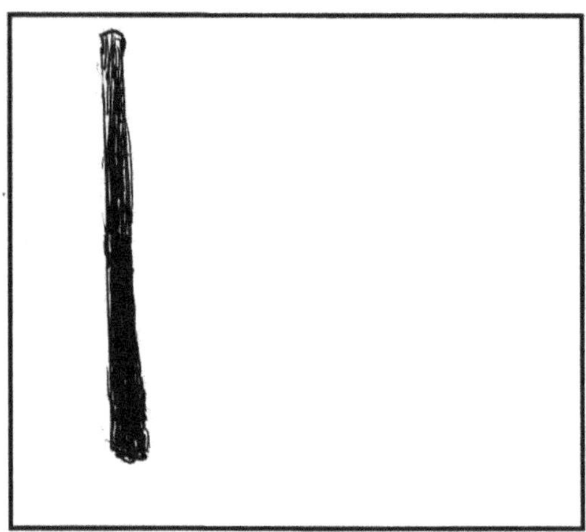

I could easily become . . .

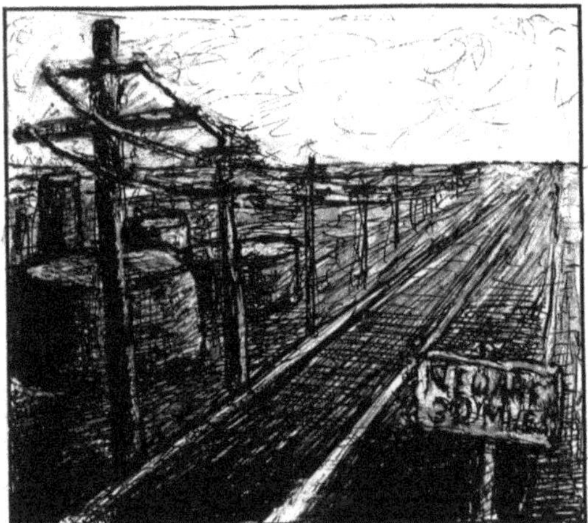

a telephone pole in New Jersey.

A line that curves like breasts or buttocks . . .

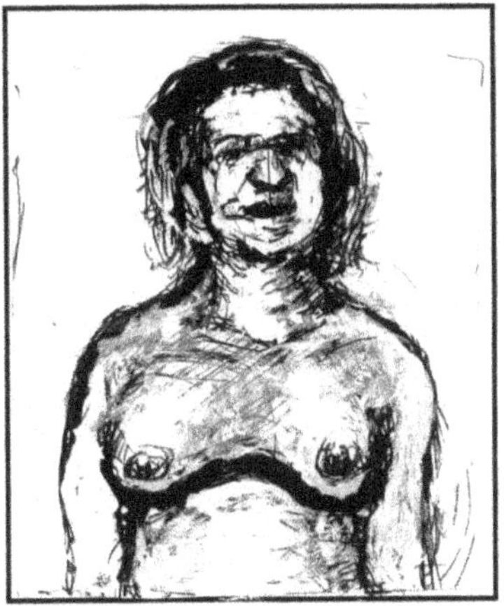

could be . . .

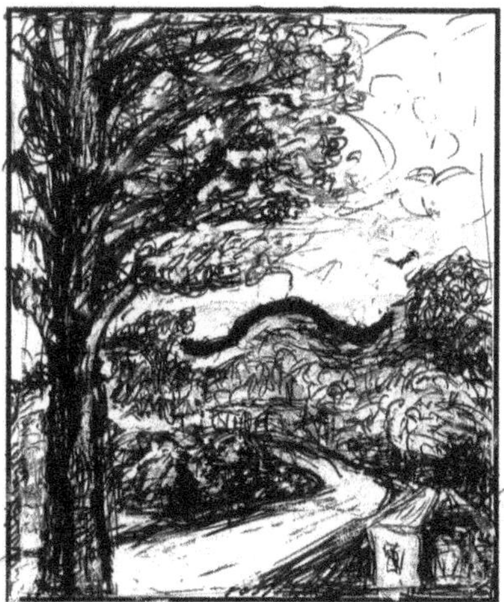

a hill in Pennsylvania.

Here's a line of scallops:

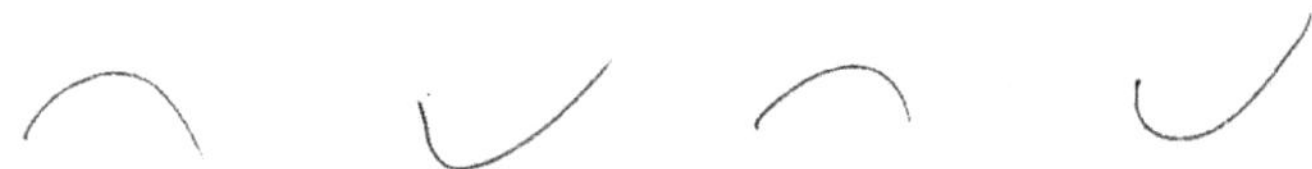

What are they? Waves? The flight path of birds? Some swoop up and some swoop down. If we put a frame around them . . .

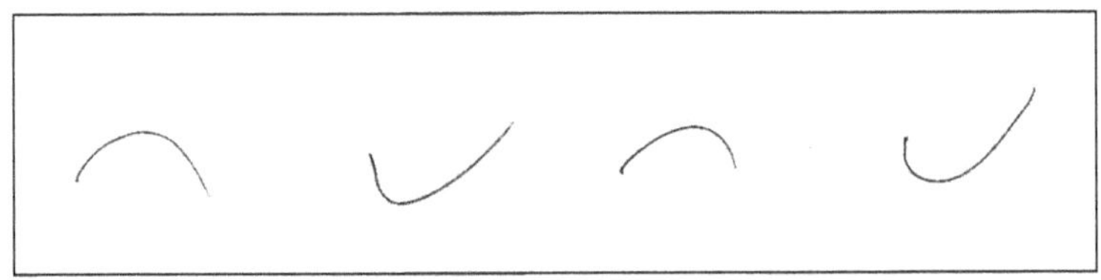

they are forced into a relationship with each other. They begin to resonate together as individual notes resonate together in a chord.

We still do not see in them as "representing" something *out there* beyond the page. In this sense they are content-less. And in this sense only they are abstractions. Asked to describe them we do not look past the forms to anything else. We find words for their shapes: "scallop," "swish," "swoop," etc.

But let us take away the frame and add some ovals:

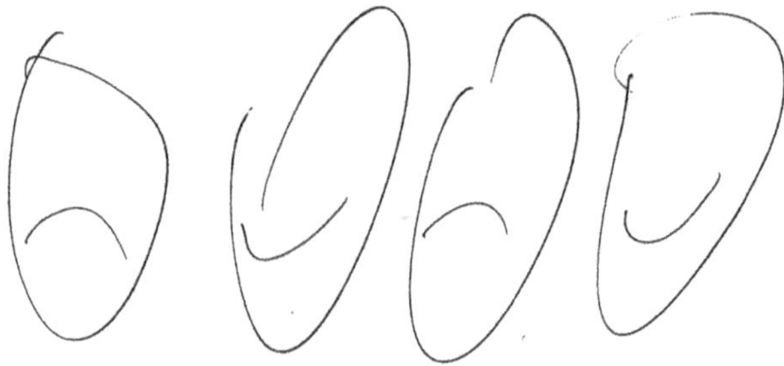

We no longer have swoops and swishes, but the beginning of . . .

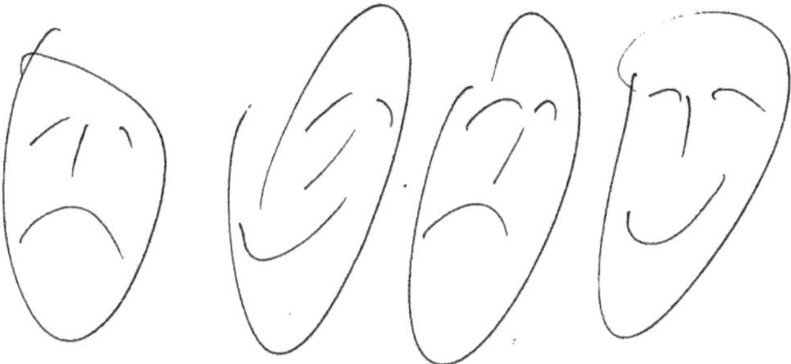

faces! Swoop and swishes be gone. Welcome smiles and frowns. We add a few more lines:

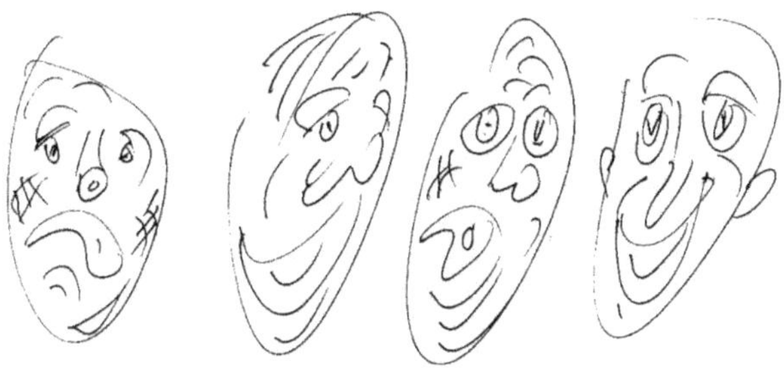

Now form and content-as-representation are pulling against each other, vying for our attention. We no longer notice forms. We see mouths and eyes—things with which we are familiar. Things we can name.

If we go further and attach heads to bodies . . .

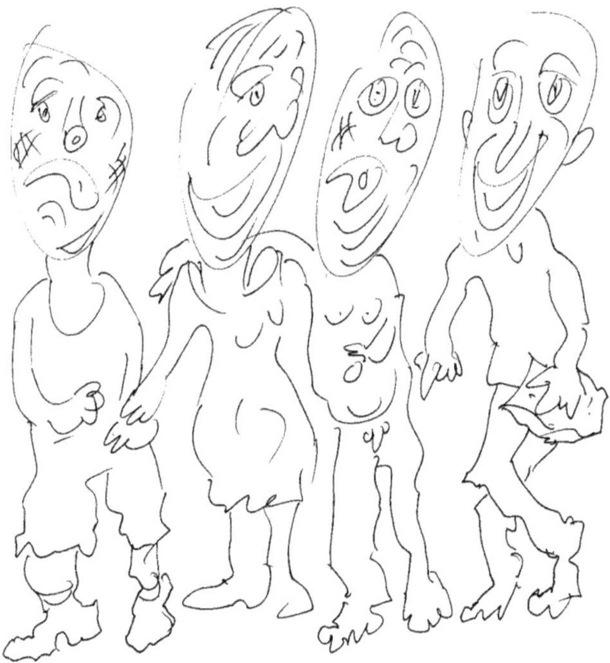

we have four people with personalities and relations to each other. Asked for a description, we will no longer be using the language of form (which has, in fact, become more complex as the drawing becomes increasingly representational). We'll tell a story about four people. One appears to be naked. One is carrying some object. Etc.

We add shading.

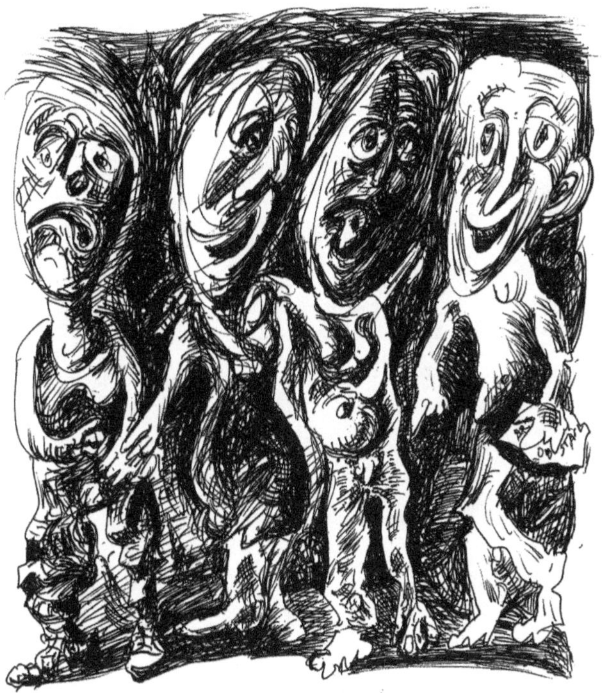

Now a whole lot is happening formally and the representational element has taken on a commensurate depth and complexity. An art teacher might gently encourage her students to notice the composition, the quality of the line, the organization of lights and darks, but she knows full well that her students will nod as if they're listening while they doodle in their notebooks.

Language requires separate conversations about the *how* and the *what.* Insofar as those conversations diverge from each other, they lead us away from the truth and meaning of the work. Returning to the work requires us to retrace our steps back to where the conversational paths diverged, which is where language falters and where form and content are restored to their irreducibly contradictory unity.

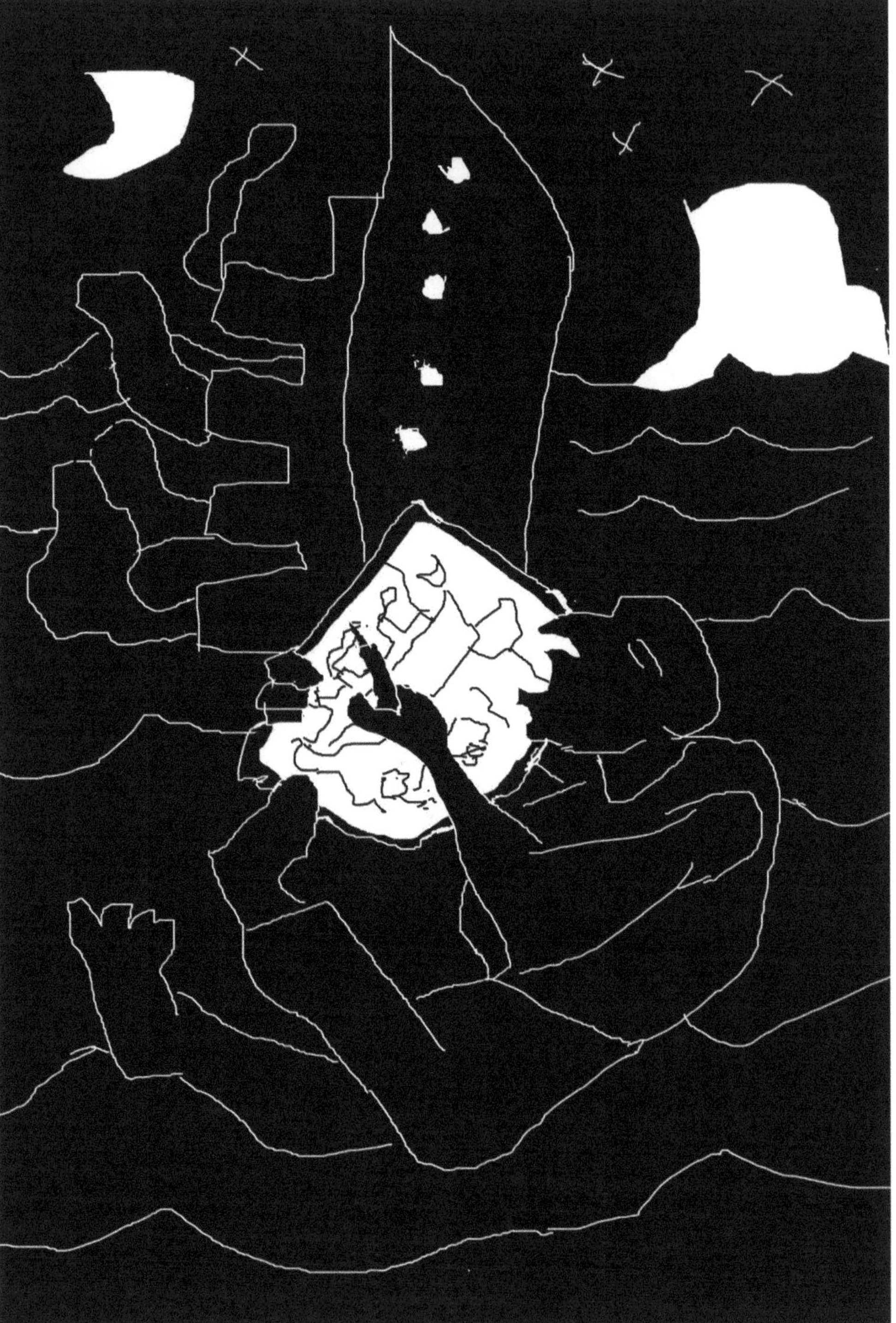

Form in Art—
The Lion Lies Down with the Lamb

ARTISTS TAKE RAW materials—paint, stone, wood—and give them a shape. Carpenters, welders, and manufacturers of automobiles also give shape to materials. But the objects they shape have a job to do in the world, and the shape they give to material is determined by the job description. The roof must keep out rain, so it can't have holes. If the cable is to hold up the bridge, it has to be thick like an arm. Thin as a thread won't do. The form of a work of art is not governed by any such external necessity. Its form has no function.*

The form of a hammer is determined by its function. A good hammer is good for pounding nails. It may incidentally be beautiful. Pausing from her work, a carpenter might find herself admiring the smoothness of its wooden handle and the complex curves of its metal head. When she retires, she may hang it on the wall and take pleasure in its beauty. Perhaps an artist friend will ask to borrow it and incorporate it in one of her assemblages. In each of these situations, the shape of the hammer does

* As we have seen, form can serve a representational "function," but whatever the external pressures may be on artists "to get a good likeness," form itself has no such requirement. Of course, it is only recently that art has obtained its independence from utility and gained recognition as a domain with its own intrinsic value. Most of the "art" that hangs in museums served religious or ceremonial or commemorative purposes. But for us, who admire it "as art," those purposes are quite irrelevant. Goya was employed by the royal family of Spain to produce portraits of kings and queens. Michelangelo painted scenes from the Bible on the ceiling of the Sistine Chapel at the behest of Pope Julius II. Rembrandt painted *The Night Watch* on commission, to decorate the hall of a company of civic militia. The original purpose that these works served—though not what they depict—is quite irrelevant to our aesthetic appreciation.

not change, but when it's used as a tool its form recedes silently into the background. Freed from utility, the mute form finds its voice. No longer in the utility belt of the carpenter, the hammer speaks for itself of its years pounding nails, just as the bent back of the laborer in retirement speaks of his years carrying heavy loads.

A hammer begins its life as a tool, puts in years of service, and may, in its old age, become a piece of art. Those objects that artists make when they set out to make a work of art are lucky exceptions to the rule that everything must have a use. They're exempt from service. But they do not leave the world of utility unacknowledged and abandoned to its fate. Edward Hopper, sketching in the evening outside an isolated gas station on a country road, is not wondering whether his tank is full. But in *Gas*, he paints the loneliness of the man attending the pumps.

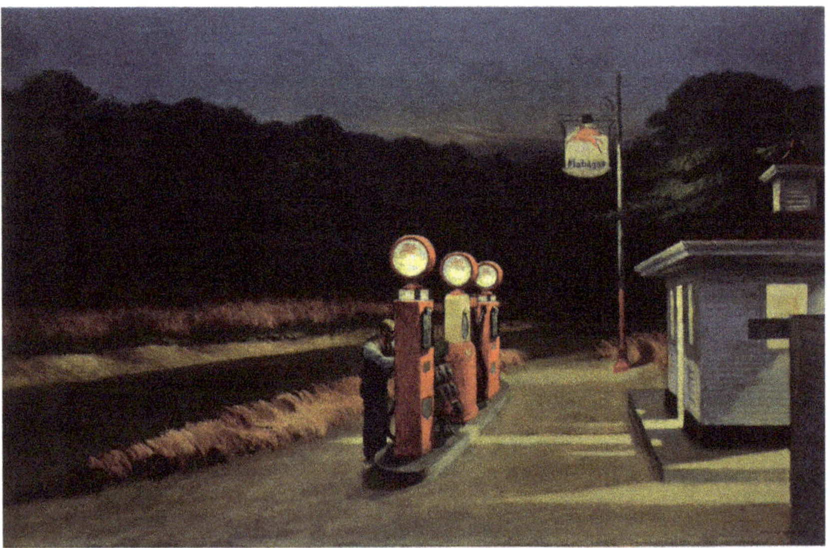

Edward Hopper, *Gas* (1940)

Van Gogh preparing to paint a worn pair of peasant boots is not worrying that they may pinch. But in his *Boots with Laces*, we feel his compassion for the hard work and poverty of the unknown laborer who wore them ragged.*

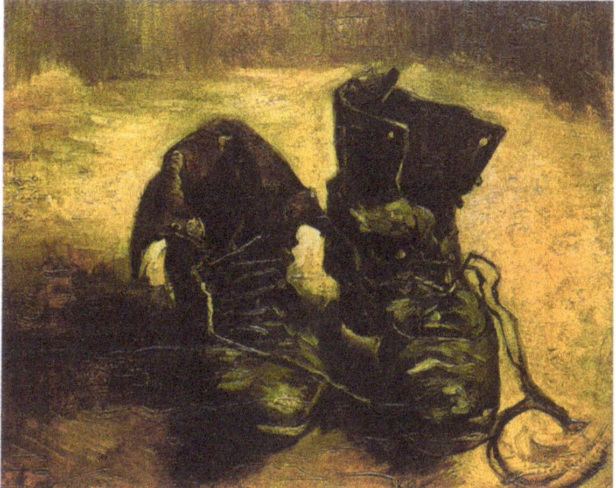

Van Gogh, *Boots with Laces* (1886)

*Whose boots were they? Most probably his own, though he may only have worn them once: A letter from Francois Gauzi, a fellow artist, describes what are most likely the boots in question:

> "At the flea market, [Vincent] had bought an old pair of clumsy, bulky shoes—peddler's shoes—but clean and freshly shined. They were fine old clonkers, but unexceptional. He put them on one afternoon when it rained and went for a walk along the old city walls. Spotted with mud, they had become interesting.. . . Vincent faithfully copied his pair of shoes."

Cited in Meyer Shapiro "Further Notes on Heidegger and van Gogh," in *Theory and Philosophy of Art: Style, Artist, and Society.* New York: George Braziller, 1994, 145.

Martin Heidegger assumed they belong to a peasant woman. He goes on at some length reading her life into them:

> From the dark opening of the worn insides of the shoes the toilsome tread of the worker stares forth. In the stiffly rugged heaviness of the shoes there is the cumulative tenacity of her slow trudge through the far-spreading and ever-uniform furrows of the fields swept by a raw wind. On the leather lie that dampness and richness of the soil. Under the soles slides the loneliness of the field-path as evening falls. In the shoes vibrates the silent call of the earth, its quiet gift of the ripening grain and its unexplained self-refusal in the fallow desolation of the wintry field. This equipment is pervaded by uncomplaining anxiety as to the certainty of bread, the wordless joy of having once more withstood want, the trembling before the impending childbed and shivering at the surrounding menace of death.

Martin Heidegger, "The Origin of the Work of Art" in *Art and its Significance: An Anthology of Aesthetic Theory*, ed. Stephen David Ross. Albany: State University of New York Press, 1994, 257-258.

The story those boots tell is locked in the form and therefore resists interpretation. All the words that escape from Heidegger's pen, are—like so much writing about art—efforts to say the unsayable.

Form is not simply external appearance; it is the mode in which objects speak for themselves. When we approach the world without the urgency to do something to it; when we have no need to cut it, chop it, masticate and mold it; when it is not grist for our mill, it opens up to us. It opens to us because we are open to it. We intend it no harm. We meet it without preconditions. This mutual opening permits us to establish relationships which bypass formalities. What is individual and unique reveals itself as universal. In the towering redwood, we discover the thrusting grandeur of the natural world; in the old man hobbling along the sidewalk, age and frailty; in the round of a bowl on the breakfast table, the fruitful promise of all rotundity; in the corpse of the tortured prisoner, the suffering of all humanity.

The work of art gives us the individual and unique—this cat sunning itself on the windowsill at eight in the morning on Tuesday; this man sipping coffee in a café in Beirut. But in a great painting this particular "cat" is the essence of catness; this coffee drinker, humanity itself. Essence shines forth. Within the peaceable kingdom of art, appearance never conceals reality. Appearance *is* reality.

If houses built themselves, if bridges sprung up spontaneously to carry us over bodies of water, if food dropped from the trees into our hungry mouths, if we did not have to work for a living, we could spend our days appreciating the beauty of the natural world. If she had no fear of being eaten, the lamb could appreciate the form of the lion—the grace of her leap, the pearly whiteness of her teeth, even her fearsome energy. If she had other means of satisfying her appetite, the lion would appreciate the soft wooliness of the lamb. If we lived in a peaceable kingdom, we could appreciate forms independent of their function.

Art is a peaceable kingdom that's mapped onto a world of suffering. The loneliness of the gas station remains in Hopper's painting; the weariness of the worker is there in van Gogh's boots. The lion lies down with the lamb but watches her hungrily. And the lamb is afraid.

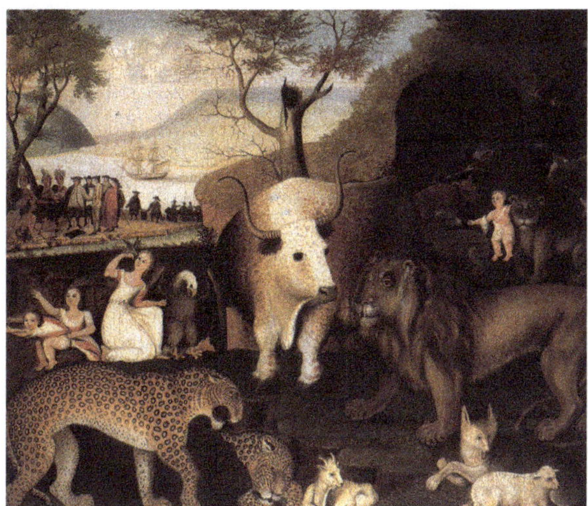

Edward Lee Hicks, *The Peaceable Kingdom* (1826)

Art is not a kingdom that allows us to forget the horror of a world that lies outside its borders. Art that was only about forgetting would be art that that left the world unredeemed. It could offer us only a tainted pleasure. Its promise of happiness would be a cruel joke.

Life today trembles on the verge of extinction. The planet boils. The seas are dying. Crops rot where hunger gnaws the belly. Prison walls conceal abominations. Screams shred the night. We need art. Life is too hard without it.

And we need a revolution. Life is too hard without one. We need both—art and revolution. We need art while we're waiting for the revolution. We'll need art during the revolution. And afterwards . . .? Would we still need art if justice rained down on earth, nature sighed in satisfaction, all the children were fed, the rich were no longer rich and the poor lived as well as they might? We would. Our existence would be much improved, but the gulf that divides us from the world would not be bridged. We would still be over here. The world would still be over there. We would not live forever; our questions would never be fully answered, our desires never entirely fulfilled, our wounds never completely healed.

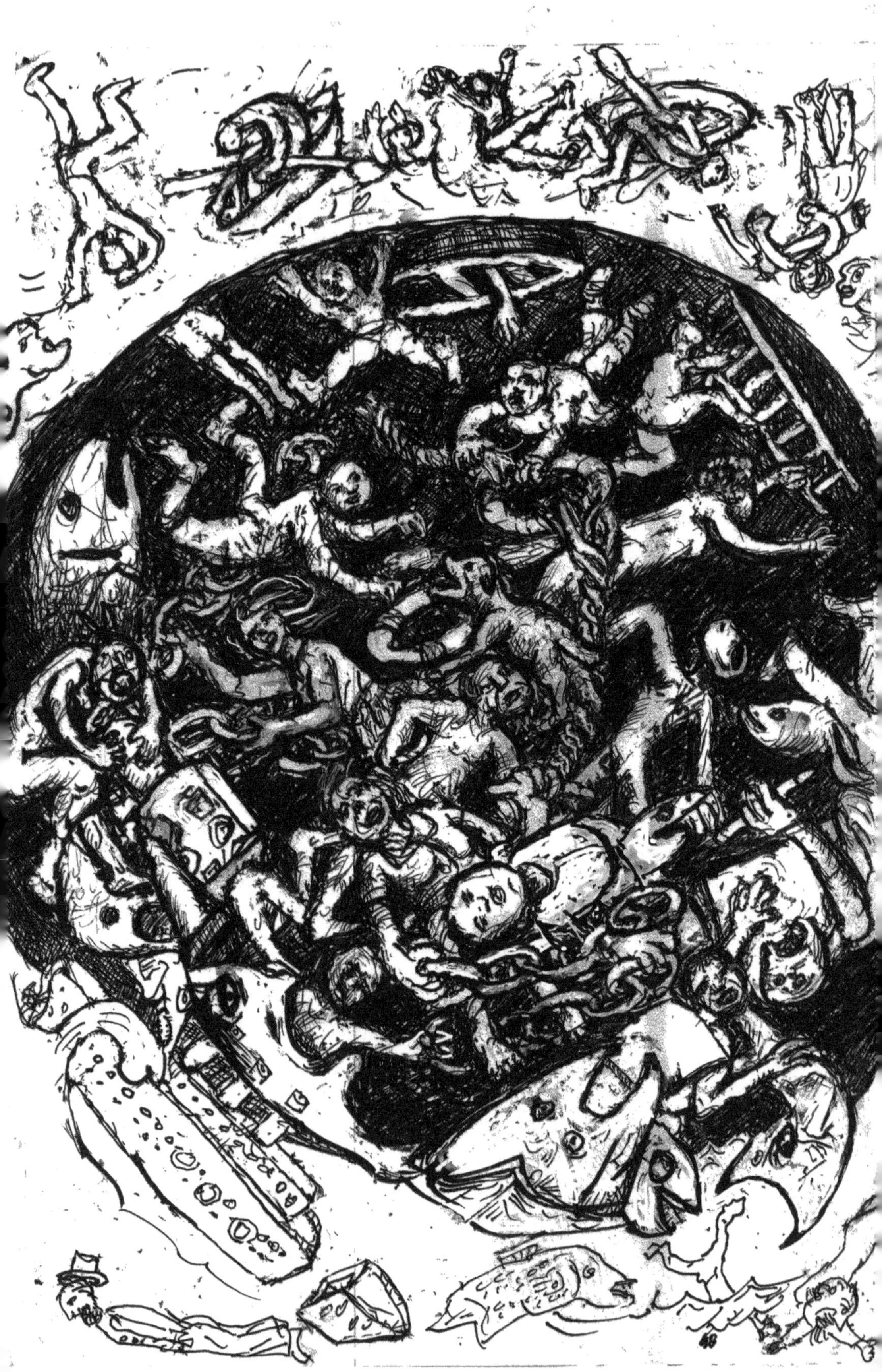

A World Apart

IN TRIBAL SOCIETIES, and in great civilizations long since crumbled into dust, images of enormous power and great beauty were created to glorify rulers and please the gods. The gorgeous objects collected in museums and reproduced in expensive coffee table books were once tools and adornments, bridges to the spirit world, and vessels of the sacred. Taken from their context and plunked down in museums, they are transformed into works of art. The masks that sit on pedestals in the galleries of African art were removed from the faces of sweaty dancers, who, for the length of the dance, embodied the spirit they represented. Like caged animals in the zoo, they retain their fearsome power, but no longer function in the world that gave them birth. They have entered a new world of quite recent invention, a world apart, the art world.

The art made before there was such a thing as art is perhaps the greatest ever made. For us it is enough that it is beautiful. But it was not created simply to be aesthetically pleasing. It had a job to do. If an object was not made in the correct manner, it was useless. The vast army of terra-cotta warriors buried in the 3rd century BCE with Emperor Qin Shi Huang stood ready to defend him in the afterlife. They are portrayed fully armed. Naked and weaponless they would have been of little use. Early Chinese statues of the Buddha were considered to be dead until brought to life "in a ceremony of 'eye opening' during which the pupils are painted in the eyes of the statute."[8] A Yoruba woodcarver designates his carving as representing an *orisha* [a Yoruba deity] by saying " 'Let this piece of wood mean . . . [the particular *orisha* it is meant to represent].' The onlooker must renew the designation. The image can be dethroned by saying: 'You mean nothing to me anymore' and then the image becomes a *kintu,* a piece of wood, which is good for nothing but kindling. . . . Hence the carelessness with which Africans treat works of art that 'no longer mean anything.' "[9]

The characteristic mask worn by dancers in rituals of Mende women's secret societies is an ebony black helmet in the shape of a woman's head, with an elaborate hair wrap and a fat, fleshy neck. The leaders of the society "have established the rules of fine form, and they insist that every mask . . . meet its high standards. . . . An incomplete mask cannot properly 'perform' in the society. . . . For a mask to be accepted . . . it must first and foremost be beautiful, enchantingly beautiful."[10] But "No matter how glorious its appearance . . . a mask that cannot be used in the dance is a piece of furniture . . . only fit for the uninitiated. Like a pretty woman with the misfortune to be barren it is considered . . . useless, empty beauty."[11]

The rise of the bourgeoisie, the formation of secular states, and the triumph of capitalism provide the context in which European art, after the fall of Greece and Rome, freed itself from service to church and state. Private citizens with disposable income supplanted prelates and princes as patrons of the arts. Art became a commodity, bought and sold on an art market. It left the palaces and sacred spaces that had been its former home and found a new sanctuary—the museum.

Once the making of art gained recognition as an activity that required freedom from the rules that govern the workaday world, works of art became worlds unto themselves. Freedom from utility became one of their defining characteristics; we learned to admire their beauty and distinguish the aesthetic pleasure we derived from them from all other pleasures of the senses. And so it is that I feel a great peace washing over me as I stare at a photograph of a Khmer Buddha, though I am no Buddhist, and I am touched by the suffering of Grünewald's tormented Christ, though I am no Christian. I take pleasure in the eroticism of slim-wasted, large breasted dancers carved on the walls of an Indian temple. In admiring these objects as "works of art," I am moved by qualities they actually possess. Their power could not possibly be a happy accident. They did not wait to be beautiful for me to approach them as art. They were made by artists who strove to create powerful, beautiful, soul-stirring objects, because only by having those qualities, which we think of as "aesthetic," could those objects fulfill the function for which they were intended.

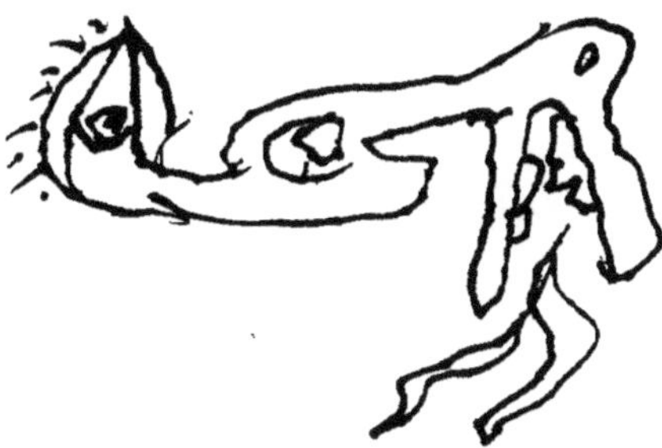

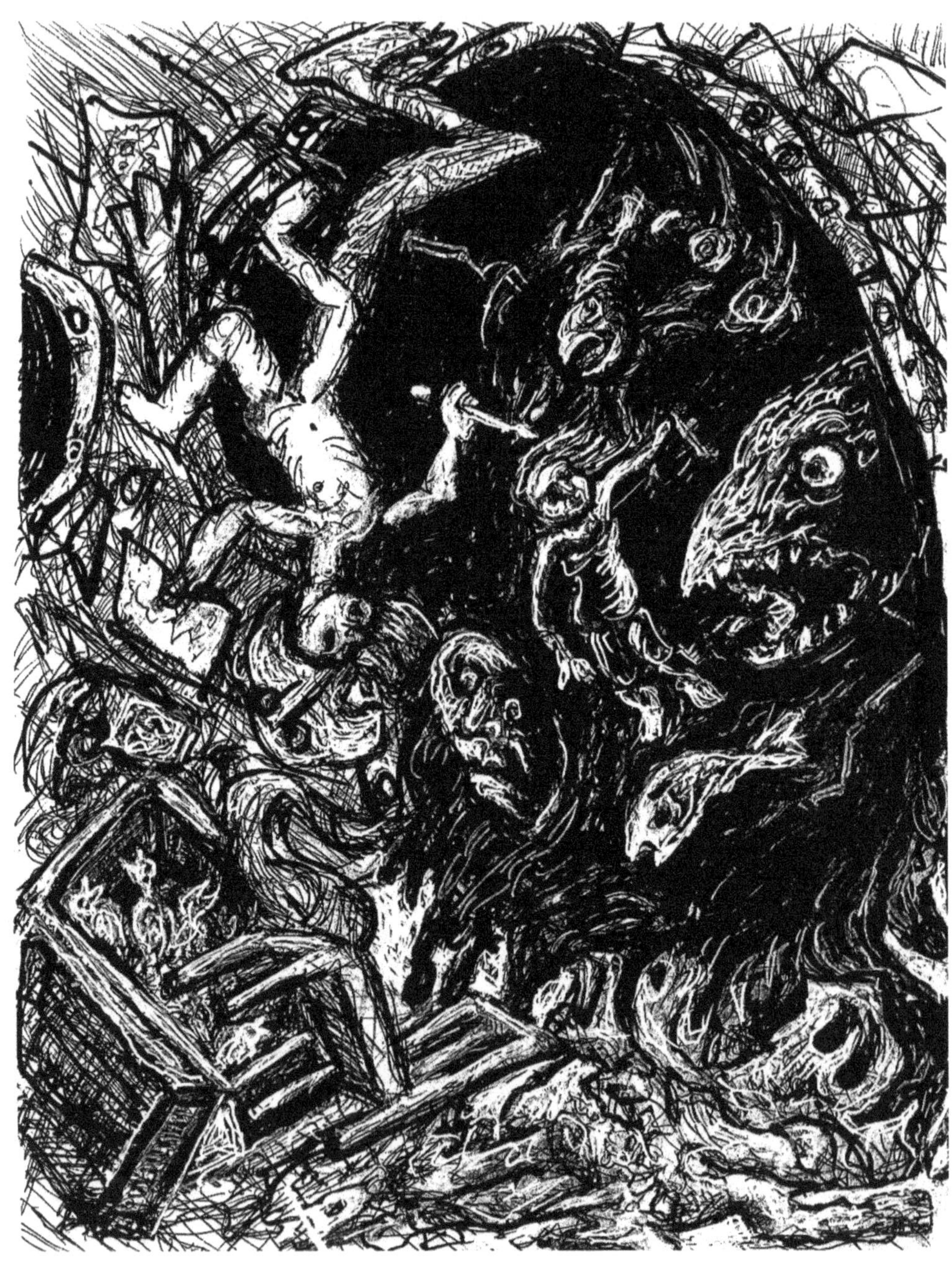

Freedom and Boundaries

A HOPI WOMAN sits by a cooking fire preparing to paint designs on a bowl. Steam rises from the stew bubbling on the flames. Children chase each other nearby. She keeps an eye on the children that they do not hurt themselves, and on the stew that it not bubble over, and the pot that must hold water. She is embedded in life. And yet I imagine that as she takes the bowl in her hands and begins to apply the paint, the emerging design pulls her away from the world. It takes command and she follows. Children, fire, and stew are left momentarily behind.

There is always a boundary between art and life, though sometimes the border is unmarked, and sometimes there is comparatively free passage from one side to the other. On the side of life is the fire that must be tended, the children that must be kept from harm, the stew that cannot be allowed to boil over. Life is a realm of necessity. It's the realm of obligations that must be met, of needs that must be fulfilled, of laws of nature that require us to breathe if we want to stay alive, and consider gravity with every step we take. It's a realm of causes that rigidly determine effects. Through the maze of necessity, freedom picks its way gingerly. On the side of art is the painting of the design. Here a different necessity rules. Here there is freedom for the hand to go where it will, constrained only by the necessity of the design—a formal necessity, seemingly unrelated to the necessity that controls the realm of life.

The bowl the Hopi potter makes must hold water. And for reasons that have nothing to do with utility, it must be beautiful. The realm of life where function matters and the realm of art where it does not remain intimately connected. Today the two realms drift apart, a chasm looms between them, and artists revel in the freedom to make objects that are militantly useless. Marcel Duchamp puts a urinal on a pedestal, calls it *Fountain,* and exhibits it in a gallery, thereby proving that anything can become a work of art once freed from slavery to utility. Duchamp's urinal is like the lucky turkey pardoned by the president on the day before Thanksgiving. The turkey was bred to be eaten, but escapes the fate of its brethren; the urinal was made to be peed in, but not a drop will touch it.*

The boundary between the peaceable kingdom of art and the workaday world is sometimes starkly apparent, as when we enter the sacred precincts of a museum; sometimes it seems not to exist at all, as when we whistle while we work; but it never entirely disappears. In the upper reaches of the art world there is always a space that surrounds a work of art. A demilitarized zone marks the border where everyday life ends and art begins. Paintings require a frame, be it gilded wood, stainless steel, or merely the edge of the stretcher to which the canvas is nailed. They are best seen against the white walls of galleries. The concert begins with silence. Quiet precedes the song. The lights in the auditorium dim when the play begins and come back on as it ends and the audience shuffles toward the exits.

Outside the palaces of high culture, we find fewer silences and white walls. Popular art forms prefer the seething street and the sweaty

* Well, maybe a drop or two. "Swedish artist Björn Kjelltoft urinated in a copy of *Fountain* at Moderna Museet in Stockholm in 1999 ("The Year's Biggest Art Event" http://hem.passagen.se/gkrantz/ett/artiklar/kjell.html). In 1993, Pierre Pinocelli, a French performance artist, urinated in a copy of the urinal and attacked it with a hammer. He attacked it again in January 2006, at the Pompidou Center (Alan Redding "Conceptual Artist as Vandal: Walk Tall and Carry a Little Hammer (or Ax)." NewYorkTimes.com, January 7, 2006). The attempted urination of Yuan Chai and Jian Jun Xi at the Tate Modern in 2000 was thwarted by a Perspex case (Paris Ionesco "Artists who have urinated in/on Duchamp's Fountain." *Artica.* September 29, 2009) http://blog.selfportrait.net/2009/09/29/artists-who-have-urinated-inon-duchamps-fountain/.

nightclub. The ghetto is their incubator. They eschew respectability—for that brief moment before they're co-opted and turned into corporate cash cows. The audience for a classical music concert remains seated throughout the performance; its silence is broken only by the occasional muffled cough. But every Sunday, the Ebenezer Baptist church across the street from my office rocks with the call of the minister and the response of the congregation as the organist strikes the first chord of a hymn and the choir stands to sing.

No one stops talking when the band takes the stage in the back of the barroom, and no one sits still when the salsa is hot. Graffiti artists have no respect, obliterating each other's work and tagging everything in sight. Giant puppets march with protestors toward lines of helmeted police. Crazed poets declaim in the subways.

The rich prefer their art corralled within well-policed boundaries. They endow museums and applaud the arrest of graffiti artists who use the walls of the city as their canvases. They dress up for the opening of the opera season and may or may not throw a quarter to the break dancer, spinning on his back on a piece of cardboard on the sidewalk in front of the theater. They listen respectfully at the symphony and complain bitterly about the boom boxes blaring hip-hop on the street outside their windows. And there are those of us who like both—the art of the museum and the art of the street; the music in the concert hall and the music with a beat.

A song that provides a rhythm for hauling and pounding makes the work go easier. The worker is not relieved by the song of his obligation to toil for his living. But if he pauses to wipe his brow and listens to the song, he is taken for a moment out of the world of sorrow into dimension of art where his sorrow is redeemed by beauty. Art has been and hopefully will always be a mooring for the drifting ship of the soul. The "I" reconciles with the "not-I" appearance with reality, truth with beauty. These reconciliations are not possible "in reality." They are possible only in the "unreal" world of art. To preserve the possibility of that reconciliation, art must maintain a boundary that separates it from experience. It can go to the dance, but it cannot get so drunk it forgets itself. The necessity of forms that characterizes a work of art can only make itself felt within a limit, and it is the necessity of forms which closes the work against the world. The paradox of form is that while it requires separation from the world, it is also through form that the separation is bridged.

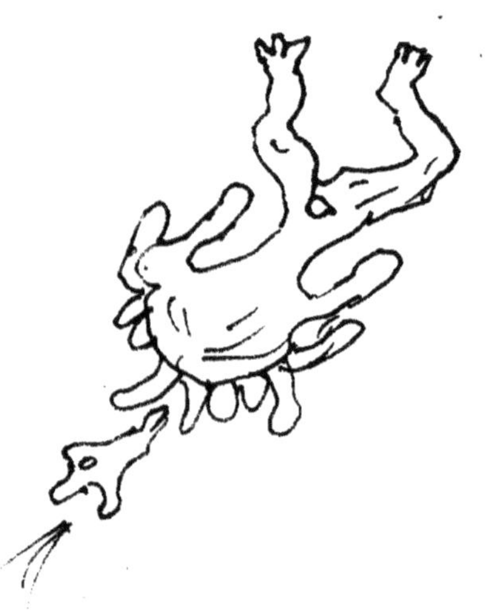

The Promise of Happiness

THE APPRECIATION OF beauty is not like other pleasures. The pleasure of a good cigar is in the smoking; of a delicious fruit, in the eating. The lover, in a night of passion, consumes her beloved. The painter merely looks.

Stendhal famously pronounced beauty to be the "promise of happiness" ("*La beauté n'est que la promesse du bonheur*"). But why only a promise? Clearly the beauty of art doesn't simply *promise* happiness. It makes us happy. And yet, at the same time, it keeps its distance from our pleasure. It is not consumed like the cigar. It doesn't dissolve into experience (although there are those who think it should).

Museums bulge with female nudes painted by men. Amorous as those men may have been, no matter how often they diddled their models, for at least as long as they were engaged in the act of painting their desire was not extinguished in ejaculation. Their hand reached for the brush, not their penis. The model in the life drawing class is for looking, not for touching (arousing as the sight of her may be). Sexuality is impatient with separation. It rushes past beauty toward an orifice or a protrusion. The centerfold in a porn magazine is for masturbation; the nude hanging in the museum is to be admired quietly in mixed company. The pleasures of art are comparatively chaste.

Pleasure dissolves distance and distance is necessary for form. Because form in art is not dissolved in pleasure, art can remain a world apart, a preserve where Stendhal's "promise of happiness" is protected from all that threatens to dash that promise *in reality*. The rebels of the world also promise happiness and endeavor to enlist art on their side. But art resists their advances and serves the revolution best by maintaining a bit of distance.

Political resistance goes hand-in-hand with cultural resistance. The great movements of social change have inspired and been inspired by a counterculture of committed artists who paint banners, design posters, write protest songs, and march alongside demonstrators in the street. In the '60s, sex, drugs, rock and roll, long hair, and opposition to the Vietnam War were all part of the mix. If art could not descend into the realm of practice, take sides in the struggle for justice, and actively take part in movements dedicated to fulfilling its promise of happiness, what use was it?

A condemned prisoner in the hours before his execution might write a poem, and would no doubt appreciate the pen and paper with which to do it, but he would certainly prefer a file to saw through the bars or a gun to shoot his way out of jail.

Art is not a file or a gun. Nor is it a mirror or a hammer. Art may contribute compelling images and rousing melodies to the struggle, but the relationship of art to politics is never easy. And it shouldn't be. Always there is a tendency for art to pull away and pursue its own agenda, an agenda determined by the work of art itself. If art submits to an agenda determined by the revolution it risks degenerating as art, and ultimately ceases to have value for politics.

Art serves the cause of human liberation by giving us an image of a world that is true to itself and deeply human. Even the slaughter of innocents, the most obscene cruelties, the worst atrocities, appear in the work of art as mastered, bound, taken prisoner by form. In its quiet or noisy way, in the hush of the gallery or the deafening decibels of the stadium concert, a work of art is revolutionary in so far as its power and beauty provides an alternative to and implicitly condemns the ugliness and brutality of the world. And the very same work of art stands *with* the world and is *not* revolutionary in so far as it accepts the limitation of the frame and thereby signals its willingness to accept the world as it is. The inability to more directly and unambiguously serve the revolution is the price art pays for its ability to resist the world and preserve the promise of a better world awaiting.

Because art does not directly take sides, it can reach across barricades. The sound of bugles leads armies into battle, but the beauty of a song rises above the conflict, and the same melody, with the words changed, can inspire either side.* The truly great works of art, no matter how fervently they were painted against their times, no matter the scandal they once provoked, eventually are accepted into the fold, and take their place, like honored elders, in the hushed galleries of the museums of the world.

The revolutionary on the barricade fights to return the world to the people. She raises her fist and shouts: "You stole our lives, our health, our happiness. You stole the wealth wrung from the earth by our sweat

* So it was with the Christmas carols that drew soldiers from their trenches to fraternize for a brief moment in no man's land before they returned to soaking the battlefields of World War I with their blood. So it has been with Beethoven's greatest symphony, as Eduardo Galeano reminds us:

> Bismarck proclaimed the Ninth an inspiration for the German race, Bakunin heard it as the music of anarchy, Engels that it would become the hymn of humanity, and Lenin thought it more revolutionary than "the Internationale." Von Karajan conducted it for the Nazis, and years later he used it to consecrate the unity of free Europe.
>
> The Ninth accompanied Japanese kamikazes who died for their emperor, as well as the soldiers who gave their lives fighting against all empires.
>
> It was sung by those resisting the German blitzkrieg and hummed by Hitler himself, who in a rare attack of modesty said that Beethoven was the true führer.
>
> Paul Robeson sang it against racism, and the racists of South Africa used it as a soundtrack for apartheid propaganda.
>
> To the strains of the Ninth the Berlin Wall went up in 1961.
>
> To the strains of the Ninth, the Berlin Wall came down in 1989.
>
> Eduardo Galeano, "The Ninth" in *Mirrors: Stories of Almost Everyone*. New York: Nation Books, 2009, 335-336.

On the other hand, art that seems safely defanged can sometimes retain its bite. United Nations officials decided that a tapestry reproduction of Picasso's *Guernica* was an inappropriate background for a press briefing by Colin Powell, who had just delivered a speech to the Security Council urging war on Iraq. The speech was filled with preposterous fabrications. The tapestry was covered with a blue curtain.

and blood. The diamonds dug from your mines belong to us who work in their dark bowels. The wheat in your sunny fields belongs to us who planted it and reaped the harvest. You have sold the fruit of our labor and pocketed the profits. We want what's ours. We've come to take the world back."

The artist also struggles to take back the world. Van Gogh struggles with the sunlight and the wheat to make it his, to appropriate it. He struggles alone, but if he succeeds, his victory belongs to all of us. His struggle is not with the bosses or the owners of the wheat field. The police will not be called when he leaves with his picture under his arm. He takes only the image, not the reality, only the hope, not its realization.

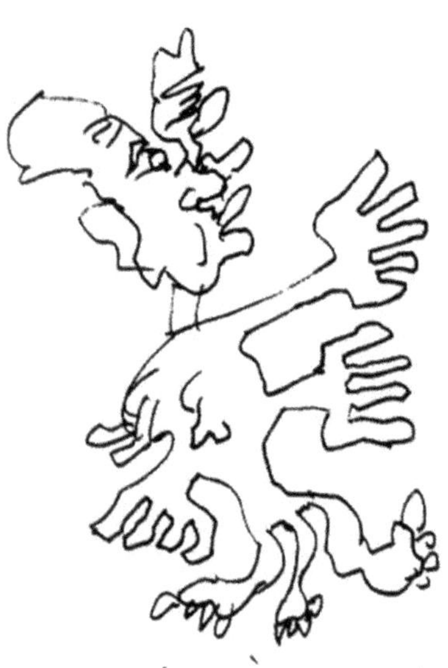

The Museum without Walls

> No trace survives of the power which called forth Egypt out of the prehistoric night; but the power which brought forth [the statue of pharaoh] Zoser from it speaks with the voice as compelling as that of the master-builders of Chartres and that of Rembrandt. With the man who made that statue we have nothing in common, not even his feelings toward such major issues as love and death not even, perhaps, the same—way of seeing his work. Yet when we contemplate the statue, the accent of a sculptor forgotten for five thousand years seems as invulnerable to the rise and fall of empires, as ageless as is the accent of maternal love.
>
> André Malraux, *The Metamorphoses of the Gods*[12]

THE BASIC STRUCTURE of consciousness is universal. Throughout history, we all wake from sleep to an awareness of being in a world we hold in common. We share that world, but each of us has an "inner world" accessible only to ourselves. The world we share and all that's in it appears to me and to you. Stuff lingers after we move on. It does not disappear when we turn our back. We only know it as content of our consciousness, but we know it's out there whether we're conscious of it or not. We're constantly bumping into it unexpectedly.

All consciousness is self-consciousness. As self-conscious beings, we lack the simple oneness of things—bottles, rocks, bicycles, bananas. Things are not self-aware. They are not aware of us. We are aware of them. Our consciousness *is* our being. When I forever cease to be conscious, I will forever cease to be.

My consciousness, which is simultaneously self-consciousness and consciousness of that which is not self, lacks rocklike unity. It is split and not split. And therefore I am split—myself and not myself, from birth to death. And so are we all.

In the work of art, that split is somehow healed. The self and the world are re-presented as if they had never been apart. Van Gogh's wheat fields are made of the sunlight and movement that fills his being as he sits squinting under his straw hat. The bodies of Michelangelo's saints, prophets, slaves, and sinners have the weight of his homoerotic longing to touch and caress the muscular bodies of the men he passes on the streets of Rome. And the bison of Lascaux surrendered their wildness to artists, whose eyes leapt to grasp their plunging flight.

In great works of art we experience a resolution of the tension between subject and object. The work of art is a safe haven where the fractious fragments of our being agree to disagree and achieve a momentary unstable peace. The truth of art is not a matter of concepts and ideas about the world; it is concrete and sensuous. We recognize the kinship of great works of art, no matter the culture from which they sprang. We appreciate art that was made in distant times and places, by people whose lives were vastly different from our own. Photographic reproductions bring the world's art to our doorstep. It's all there, cheek by jowl: a carved paddle from New Guinea, an Italian Renaissance Pieta, a smiling Bodhisattva from the jungles of Cambodia, a Dadaist's urinal. We live in André Malraux's "museum without walls," an imaginary museum in whose every room we can find art that takes our breath away. What better proof can there be that something universal lies at the heart of all the art that's ever been made, at all times and all places?

Does this mean that art exists apart from history, untouched by time? Not at all. We can recognize the universal in works of art and also see them as the expression of a culture rooted in time and place. Art has a history. It bears the marks of its birth. Rembrandt would not be painting Rembrandts if he were alive today. Perhaps he'd be making movies. Only a Gabon wood carver could produce a Gabon mask; only Olmec sculptors could carve the colossal helmeted basalt heads, in whose imperious gaze we sense the might of a vanished civilization.

The Gabon tribesperson and the Wall Street financier both bump against objects which disappear from view when they turn and walk away. Both assume they do not disappear altogether, but remain, unseen, ready to be seen again. Both share their world with other people, who, like rocks and bottles, appear to have their own autonomous existence, but who, unlike rocks and bottles, have an inaccessible "interior" that is part of their world, not ours. The sky is a dome above Wall Street as it is above the market places of Oaxaca, Ankara, and Nairobi. And everywhere there is earth beneath our feet. We are born and we die. The otherness of the world is part of our condition. The tables and chairs in the board rooms of corporations, like the rocks and flint instruments of a neolithic village, are outside of and indifferent to our kaleidoscopic inner life. And yet our experience of self and world, of self and not-self is profoundly historical. The fundamental relation of self to world, of the "I" to the "not-I," holds a tension that increases and decreases in response to changes in how we live with each other and with the object world that surrounds us. The relation of who we are to what we are not has a history that we can we read as we walk through the galleries of Malraux's museum without walls. Is the world out there hostile, alien, or the self writ large? Do we live embedded in family or interred in a prison camp? Do we see the stars at night or only the glow of street lamps? Is there a living unity, a common spirit which includes us as it includes the birds, the sky, and the children playing by the river bank? Or has that unity been shattered? Is the world knowable or not? Is our relationship to the world assured and managed by gods or is the universe empty of assurances?

How fast are things?
How bright?
Is stone the metaphor?
Or light?

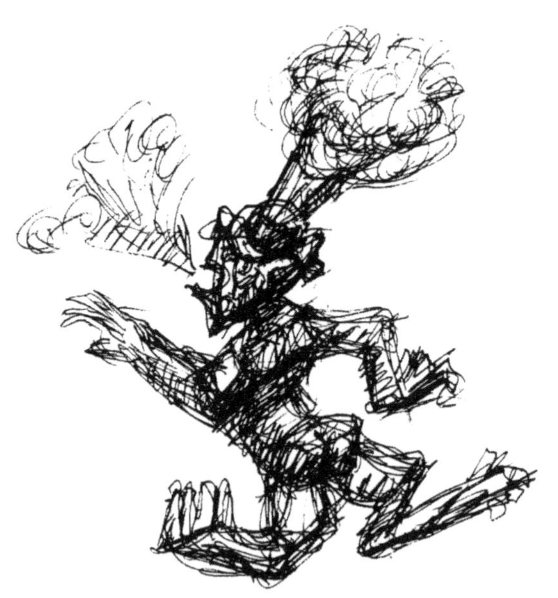

I Teach Art History and Come to a Sweeping Conclusion: Things Fall Apart

I FIRST STUDIED art history at Swarthmore College in the late '50s. The class met early in the morning; the professor would dim the lights to show slides and soon I would be sound asleep. I did, however, stay awake long enough to learn that the professor saw the history of art in a linear progression culminating in the modern art of Europe and the United States. No mention was made of the art of China or Japan. Once we moved past Egypt, Sumer, and Assyria, Africa and the Middle East dropped off the map (and since Egypt was never discussed as an African civilization, in a sense Africa never made it onto the map at all). Later, after I dropped out of Yale to become a painter, I briefly taught art history at the School of Visual Arts in Manhattan. With a few embellishments, what I taught was based on what I learned at Swarthmore. My course followed the history of art through the centuries, beginning with Lascaux and ending with the art that was being shown at the time in the trendy midtown New York galleries. I showed slides that I checked out from the main branch of the New York Public Library. I loved the way paintings looked, enlarged and illuminated by the light of the projector. Small details, many times their original size, became independent works of art, which in many cases I preferred to the originals.

As I watched one formal universe give way to the next, it occurred to me at some point that the succession of slides I was showing was like the vapor trail in a cloud chamber left by the passage of subatomic particles. I was seeing the visible mark of invisible events in the relation of consciousness to itself and to the world. Each painting or sculpture could be seen as an answer to a set of questions: What is the relationship of appearance to reality? Do appearances reflect reality or conceal it? For that matter, what is real? Are space and time experienced as seamless, or fragmented and discontinuous? Is there a coherent, comprehensible relation between the self and the world, or is that relationship fraught with disconnects and contradictions? What is the experience of the self that people had in the past? Is it analogous to my own or different in ways I can not imagine?

I knew my students were not particularly interested in these questions, so I tried little tricks to keep them awake. In our first class I had them cut up postcards of the *Mona Lisa* and reassemble them into a collage. I hoped to make a point about art in the age of mechanical reproduction. But I also thought I could use it to demonstrate the gulf that separated the world in which Leonardo labored for years to preserve the smile of the Mona Lisa and 20th-century America where my students were chopping up her image. Mechanical reproduction made possible the supply of twenty-five cent postcards that my students happily sliced and diced. But the availability of cheap copies did not create the shift in consciousness that allowed us to see the aesthetic possibilities in the destruction and dismemberment of images.

Iconoclasm has a long history. For millennia, the statues of deposed rulers have been torn from their pedestals. Their faces have been chiseled from the temples they erected; portraits of hated dictators have been slashed and trampled by the crowds that swept them from power. The attack on the image is an attack on what it represents. The *Mona Li*sa has been a particularly tempting target. She hangs in the Louvre, a dull brownish green painting, protected by bulletproof glass. Any possibility of seeing her afresh has been destroyed by overfamiliarity. The impulse to mess with her seems to be irresistible. She has survived a number of acts

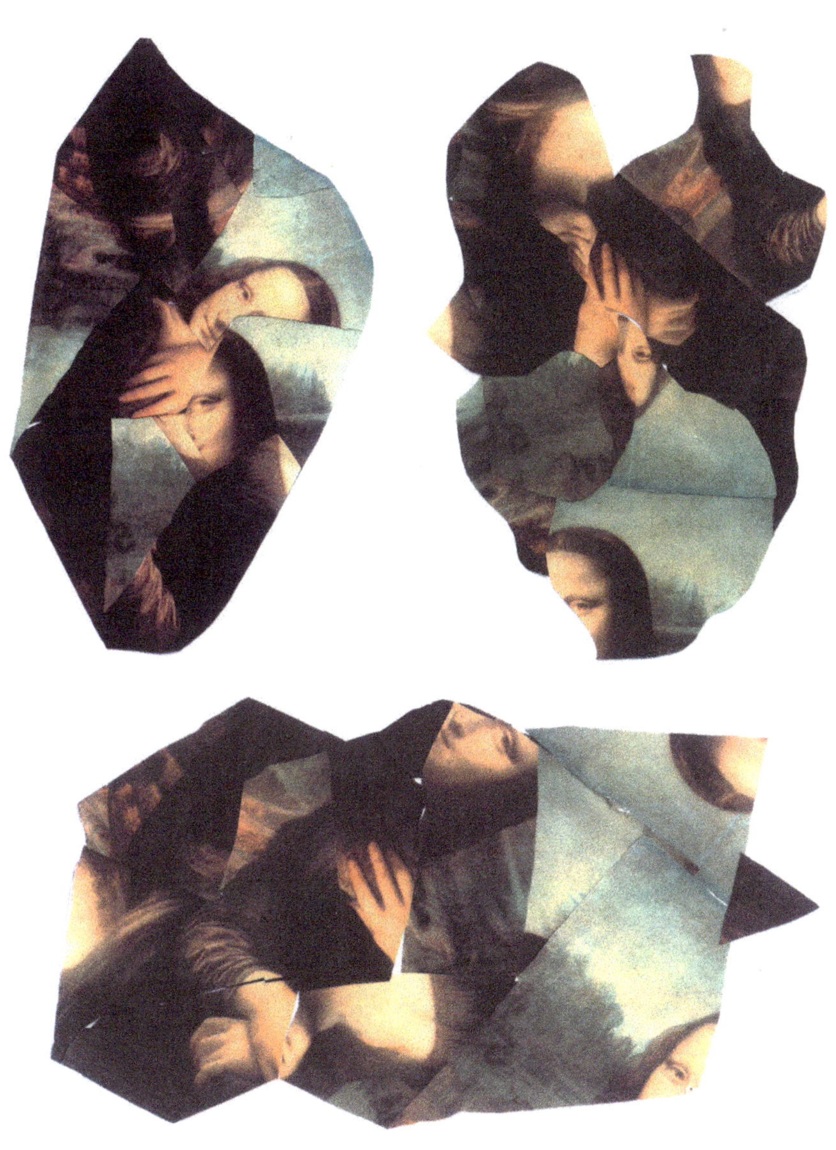

The Mona Lisa sliced and diced

of vandalism.* The animus against her may have a misogynistic component. A battering husband will hit his wife to wipe the enigmatic smile off her face. Nevertheless, it's not Ms. Lisa; it's the *Mona Lisa,* the too famous painting that inspires our hostility. I asked my students to notice the pleasure they take in her—its—dismemberment, and to consider that the destruction of form and all its embedded content has become, in the 20th century, a central component of the artistic process. I said we all share a modern aesthetic that distrusts the illusions of conventional representation and prefers the fragmentary and dissonant to the unified and harmonious aesthetic universes achieved by the geniuses of the Italian High Renaissance.

How long had that change in our aesthetic been in preparation? What did it signify? I thought I could detect, in the succession of slides I showed each week in my class, the gradual dissolution of the coherent world view that was the basis of Renaissance art. Of course, art does not march forward single file. A pull in one direction is often countered by a push in the opposite. In the course of a single lifetime, an artist may begin by carefully subjecting herself to the discipline of objects and end by living fully in an aesthetic universe of her own devising. In their old age, the truly great artists—Michelangelo, Titian, Goya, Rembrandt, Monet—faced the final pulling apart of self and world by creating works in which the world of resistant objects surrenders entirely to their subjectivity. Art may perpetually cycle between the poles of subject and object,

*In 1956, she was badly damaged in an acid attack. (BBC News Faces of the Week, September 29, 2006). On December 30 of that same year, a young Bolivian, Ugo Ungaza Villegas, threw a rock at her. This resulted in the loss of a speck of pigment near her left elbow, which was later restored (http://www.monalisamania.com/faq.htm). In April 1974, in Tokyo, a woman upset about lack of access to the Japanese National Museum for people with disabilities, sprayed red paint on the bulletproof glass protecting her. (*Sarasota Herald Tribune*, April 21, 1974 "Mona Lisa Undamaged, Still Smiling After Spray Attack in Tokyo") On August 2, 2009, a Russian woman threw a tea cup at her, which the woman had bought a few minutes earlier at the museum gift shop. The *London Telegraph* reported that "Doctors were trying to assess whether she [the woman, not the *Mona Lisa*] was suffering from Stendhal Syndrome, a rare condition in which often perfectly sane individuals momentarily lose all reason and attack a work of art." (Telegraph.co.uk August 11, 2009)

but it appeared to me that the wheel of European art, as it has cycled since the Renaissance, wobbles toward a fork in the road from which the path of the self and the path of the world increasingly diverge.

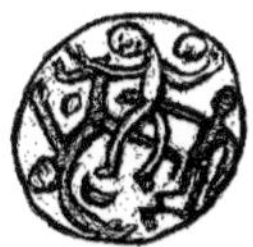

It is impossible to imagine Leonardo finding aesthetic possibilities in the tearing up of images. He began painting the *Mona Lisa* in 1503. According to Vasari, he "lingered over it four years," and still could not finish it. He carried it with him to France where he is thought to have worked on it for an additional three years, completing it shortly before he died in 1519. All that time, he labored to marry the placid portrait of a very real Mona Lisa, who sits on a patio with her arms crossed, to an imaginary landscape of forbidding crags and valleys where no one seems to live and roads wind to nowhere. He softened slightly the edges of all his forms and bathed foreground and background in a continuous flow of infinitely graded light and shadow, thereby creating a seamless world, unified in space and time, and suffused with his subjectivity. This seamless illusory universe, in which the world is re-presented as wholly known and knowable, seems today so conventional and unremarkable that it is difficult to see it as a revolutionary achievement. It has become a burdensome convention against which we fight to recover reality.

For the greater part of the history of art, any uncertainties in the relationship between the self and the world were resolved by reference to a supernatural realm of gods and spirits. The tribal art of Africa and the Pacific Islands; the art of dynastic Egypt and Mesopotamia; the classic art of India and Cambodia; and the masterpieces of the Mayan, Aztec, and Inca empires depict a transcendent world beyond appearances, where the pesky buzz of temporal existence fades into stillness. One can sometimes find in the art of ancient empires precisely observed depictions of daily life—the artists of dynastic Egypt produced delightful images of domestic life, work, and leisure—but they are subordinate elements in an art whose constant reference point is the beyond. Pharaohs, gods, and goddesses are treated with a rigid formality that removes all traces of individuality.

After centuries of art absorbed in the depiction of eyebrows, dimples, and the shine on the skin of an apple, the masterpieces of an art that bypass appearances to reach a transcendent reality seem surprisingly "modern" and "abstract."

In the *Mona Lisa* there is no hint of a split between nature and the supernatural. We do not sense a gulf between a reality that appears, and a super-reality, beyond, behind, and above the world of appearances. Leonardo is a scientist as well as an artist. What he seeks in appearances is not the revelation of the supernatural, but reality itself. He wants to know how things work. Like his contemporary Michelangelo, he dissects cadavers. He studies anatomy in order to be able to draw, and he draws in order to understand anatomy. He studies nature in order to understand the forces that shape mountains and determine the course of rivers, and he uses the sketches he makes in his studies as the basis for the landscape he paints in the background of the *Mona Lisa.*

The knowledge that Italian Renaissance artists obtained from their investigations of nature was used to depict figures with mass and weight that were confident of their place in the world and stood in harmonious relation with each other. Their anatomical studies enabled these artists to visualize the body as a rhythmic coordinated whole. Their interest was not, however, in achieving a mere surface realism, though they made great strides in the depiction of appearances. They were inspired by their rediscovery of the classical art of Greece and Rome in which gods and goddesses are depicted as exemplifying the essential truth and beauty of which our far-from-perfect bodies are but the palest shadow. In classical art, the realm of the gods is no longer inaccessible and other. It is the perfect template from which the world of appearances is struck. Beauty

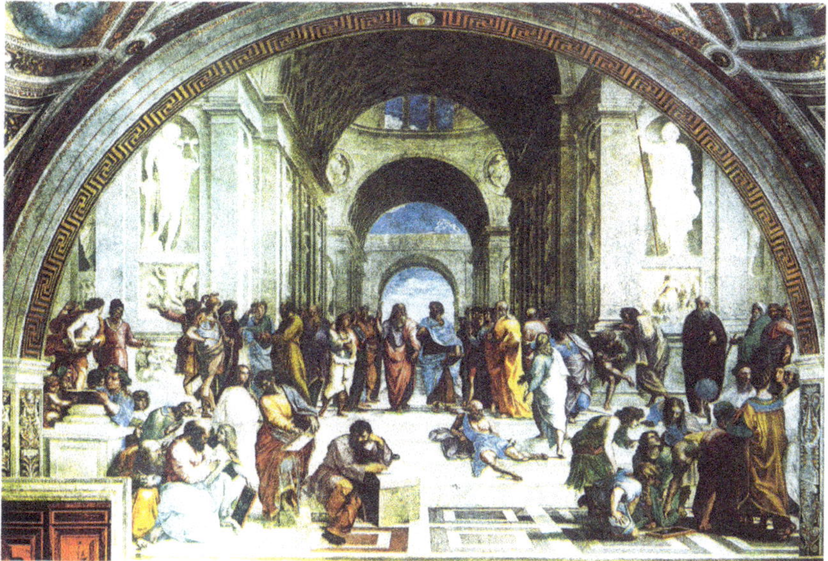

Raphael, *School of Athens* (1510-1511)

in heaven is no different from beauty on earth, and mortals can strive to be as beautiful as gods.

For a brief moment Italian Renaissance artists created ideal worlds in which all the stuttering reality of everyday life gives way to a fluid stately promenade of forms. The promenade takes place in a space tamed and stabilized by perspective. All things receded in perfect order from the eye of the artist. These ideal worlds are truer, more real, more beautiful than reality itself. In the realm of the ideal, reason prevails, appearance and reality are one.

The problem with ideal worlds is they tend to be lifeless—too perfect, static, and unblemished. But in the turbulent, warring, faction-ridden world of Renaissance Italian city states, the classical ideal was reinterpreted by artists who were conscious of themselves as unique, autonomous individuals. In their work, the stillness and perfection of the ideal is broken by ther force of their powerful personalities. A balance is struck between reason and passion, tranquility and strenuous exertion.

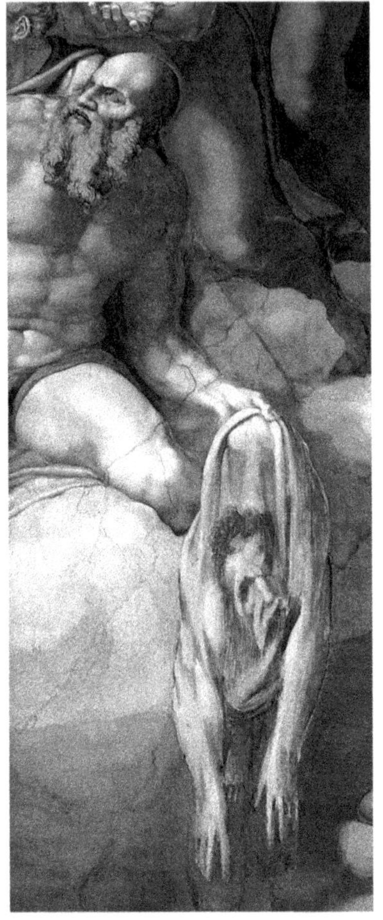

Michelangelo, *The Last Judgement* (detail) (1534–41)

Raphael's aesthetic universe may be a little too sedate for our taste. The philosophers in the *School of Athens* never lose their composure. But in Michelangelo's Sistine Chapel ceiling, prophets, sibyls, Old Testament patriarchs, naked boys, and God himself twist, shout, and lunge from the architectural frame that would contain them.

Michelangelo is a transitional figure. He is the towering self-confident representative of the high Renaissance, in whose work the mind in its majesty is revealed in the muscular radiance of the flesh. But he is also the artist who, in his last works, renounces all that majesty and radiance to plunge deeper into the torments of the soul and body.

The ideal represents an aspiration for a state of being that transcends the chaotic disorder of reality. It is always threatened from without—the more chaotic the reality, the greater the threat. Between when Michelangelo climbs down from the scaffold having completed the Sistine Chapel ceiling and when he ascends again to paint the *Last Judgment,* his world is profoundly altered. Martin Luther posts his 95 theses on the door of the Castle Church of Wittenberg. Three years later he is excommunicated. And then, in 1527, Rome is sacked by mutinous troops of the Holy Roman Empire. Nuns are raped, palaces are plundered. The Swiss Guard is slaughtered on the steps of St. Peter's Basilica, and the Pope flees for his life from the Vatican in an underground corridor.

In the *Last Judgment,* Michelangelo paints a *memento mori* for an age of anxiety. He shatters the synthesis of order and energy he had created on the Sistine Chapel. He jettisons perspective. He paints tangled clumps of figures that writhe in a space that lacks all coordinates. He paints himself as the flayed skin of Saint Bartholomew. He is no longer proud of the flesh. His body is a prison from which his spirit is released.

After the Renaissance, art enters into a period of uncertainty and anxiety known as Mannerism. Mannerism is more a mood than a style. It is post-Renaissance as today's art is post-modern. In some cases artists retain the ideal rounded forms of the Italian Renaissance but distort them as Surrealists distorted the forms they inherited from academic realism. In the work of other artists, such as El Greco, rounded forms go up in flames. Figures stretch and spin, their clothing flying and flaring in windstorms of emotion. In northern Europe, Brueghel chooses to paint scenes from everyday life. He draws with an angular line and eye for detail that harks back to a Northern Renaissance that never embraced the classical ideal.

In the Baroque, new syntheses emerge, but the unity of appearances and reality that is taken for granted by the artists of the Italian Renaissance is broken. The Baroque's discovery "that a rolling wheel loses its spokes when experienced subjectively, implies a new worldview for the 17th century."[12] The wheel "experienced subjectively" diverges from the wheel as it is "in reality."

When Frans Hals paints the lace cuffs of the Dutch burghers who have commissioned him to do their portraits, he does not, like his Northern Renaissance predecessors, attempt to depict each intricate fold of fabric. Nor, like the masters of the Italian Renaissance, does he have before him an ideal of harmony that guides his every brushstroke. He slashes quick brushloads of paint, one on top of the other. At a distance, the brushstrokes disappear and we see the frothy lace. The lace exists only in the eye of the beholder. Step close to the canvas, the lace is gone, and the brushstrokes reappear. They are the record of his gestures, the expression of his physical and mental energy. The artist appears and the world disappears. Hals' art is more "subjective" than that of his Renaissance predecessors. He paints the impression an object makes on the eye, not the object itself. But in dissolving objects into impressions, he paradoxically asserts the painted surface as an object that does not disappear. When we move close to the painting to see how the illusion is created, we encounter the surface itself as a painted plane in its opaque and stubborn material solidity. We can no longer look through it, as through a windowpane, into a space which is the space of our shared social world.

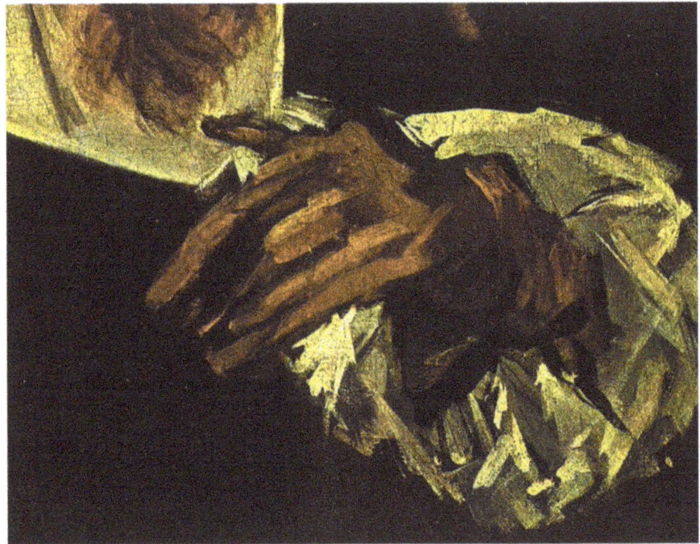

Frans Hals, *Regents of the Old Men's Almshouse* (Detail) (1664)

In Catholic countries, where the principal patrons of Baroque painters such as Rubens are princes and prelates, art glorifies and flatters rulers. Rubens' manner is heroic and idealizing. But in Protestant and republican Netherlands, artists paint for the bourgeoisie. Hals' customers want to be represented as they see themselves, and he obliges them. The tension that is developing between subjective impression and objective truth has not reached the point where it threatens the ability of painting to portray a world that is shared and familiar.

By the time I finished teaching the Baroque, I was running out of time in the semester, so I jumped over the delicate and decorative Rococo, beloved by courtiers whose heads would roll in the French Revolution. The revolutionaries who led them to the guillotine would have no use for the Rococo's courtly frills and foppery. The austere neo-classicism of David was more in tune with their republican values.

After the Revolution, classicism quickly degenerates into sentimental idealism. The life goes out of it and I spent little time discussing it. The mainstream of art, henceforth and until the modernism of the 20th century, will be committed to one form or another of realism. But what is real? Artists are increasingly faced with a choice: paint the world as it appears or as we know it to be; paint the "impression" it makes on us and the passion it invokes, or attempt to reach past passion and impressions to the thing itself; paint fantasies and hallucinations which represent the reality that reason refuses to recognize, or the hard facts of daily life that the comfortable beneficiaries of privilege would rather deny. Artists who identify themselves as romantics and those who take up the banner of realism have different answers. For Delacroix, the quintessential Romantic, "Nature is only a dictionary" to be consulted as needed by an imagination seething with visions of "desolation, massacres, conflagrations . . . eternal and incorrigible barbarism."[14]

For Courbet, the sweaty proletarian realist and revolutionary socialist, "Painting is an essentially concrete art, and can consist only of representation of real and existing things."[15]

Delacroix, by the richness of his color and the impetuousness of his brushstrokes; and Courbet, by taking everyday life as his subject matter, prepare the way for Impressionism. And both paint "impressionistically" as compared with their neoclassical counterparts in the Academy.

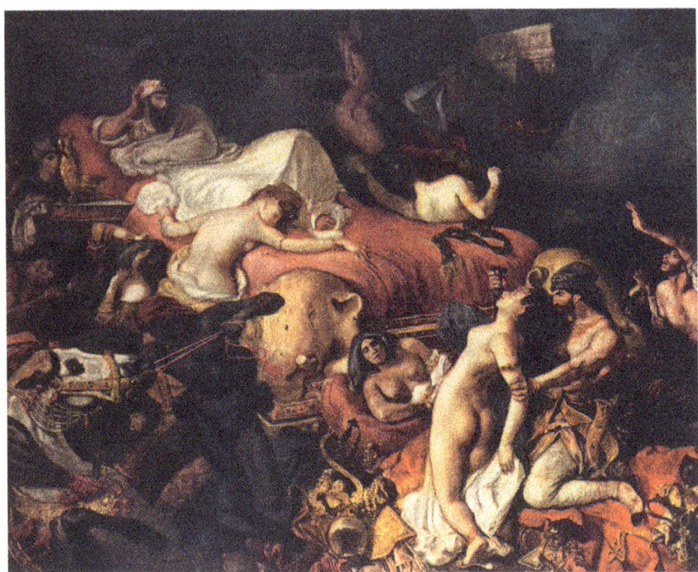

Eugéne Delacroix, *Death of Sardanapalus* (1828)

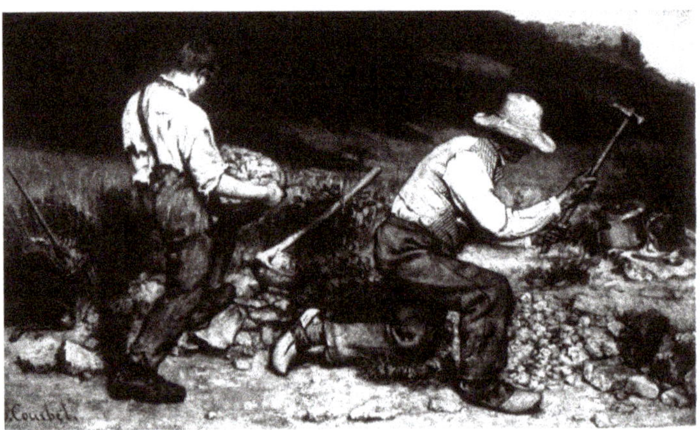

Gustave Courbet, *The Stone Breakers (*1849)

For the Impressionists, what is "real and existing" are not the concrete "things" toward which Courbet struggled in his painting, but the impact they make on the sense of sight. "The older I become," wrote Monet, "the more I realize that I have to work very hard to reproduce what I search for: the instantaneous. The influence of the atmosphere on the things and the light scattered throughout."[16] The next year he set up his easel in front of a second-floor window opposite the Rouen cathedral and began to paint. In Monet's thirty-one paintings of that cathedral, the solid mass of time-resisting stone disappears in a blizzard of vibrating light. He gives us a sunny-day cathedral; an overcast-day cathedral; a morning, midday, afternoon, and evening cathedral.

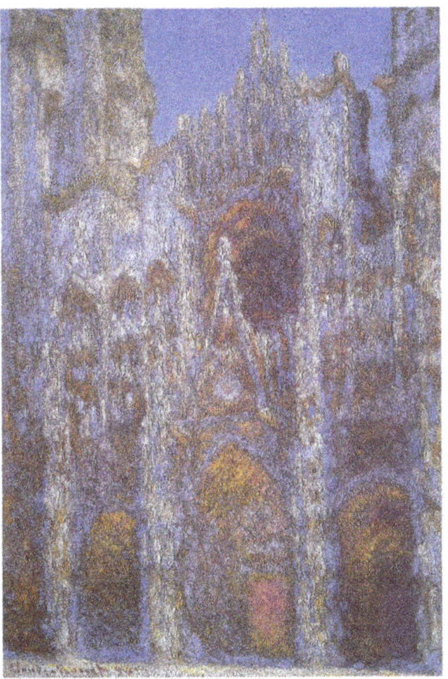

Monet, *Rouen Cathedral, Morning* (1894)

Viewed close up, Monet's canvases are covered with indecipherable daubs of color. No lines or shapes are visible; there are no boundaries to things. Monet does not attempt to convey what we know about the world by touching it, lifting parts of it, working in it, and encountering its physical resistance. We will never know from Monet the solid, permanent Rouen Cathedral of the stone masons, bricklayers, and hod carriers who built it; nor the cathedral as it is known by the souvenir vendor who hawks her wares in its shadow. Monet places himself apart from those who must heave and haul and adjust their bodies to the weight of the objects they encounter. He dissects "seeing" the way Renaissance artists dissected cadavers. Sitting by the bedside of his dying wife, he realized with horror that he has been lost in the contemplation of the colors her skin turned as her life drained away.[17]

Monet writes to his friend George Clemenceau, "I have always observed what the world showed to me, only to give testimony of it in my paintings."[18] But Monet does not reach beyond the impression to the "real and existing things" that Courbet sought to capture with his brush. He does not concern himself with the world we share that lies "beyond" or "behind" appearances. Hals made use of the optics of seeing to convey to the viewer the impression of a solid lace cuff; his art does not call the solidity of that cuff into question. There *is* a cuff, no doubt about it. Monet is not using a trick of perception to make us think we are seeing the intricate stone work of a Gothic cathedral. He dispels the illusion that we have direct access to an independently existing solid object.

Once Impressionists place a veil of fleeting visual sensations between us and the object, the question arises how contact can be reestablished. The impressions things make on us belong to the sphere of the self. How does one reach outside of that sphere toward the world?

Van Gogh paints at an agonizing point of transition to a modernism that admits its failure to bridge the divide between subject and object, the "I" and the "not-I," and accepts its inability to depict things as they are and as they appear. Van Gogh longs to be successfully married to the world, to hold on to it and bring it onto the canvas, but he is drawn by his intense emotion toward colors that take on a life of their own and forms that eddy and swirl in ecstatic delirium.

Cézanne's emotional turmoil is less well known than van Gogh's. He does not ride his emotions toward objects; he seeks to escape his inner life by concentrating his attention on objects as they exist apart from him, solid and self-contained. Where van Gogh is impetuous, Cézanne is judicious and so hemmed in by thought that it is reported he sometimes took hours to put down a single stroke of paint. Like van Gogh, he desperately pursued the real, going so far as to deny to Emile Bernard that there was a difference between art and nature. Contrasting his art to that of the classical artists, whose work fills museums, Cézanne proclaimed, "They created pictures; we are attempting a piece of nature."[19] He sought the structure lost in the dizzying buzz of photons bouncing towards the eye of the Impressionist. He said, "I want to make of Impressionism something solid and lasting like the art in museums."[20] He famously advised Emile Bernard, "treat nature by means of the cylinder, the sphere, the cone,"[21] but admitted to his friend, the painter Joachim Gachet, "Everything I am telling you about—the sphere, the cone, cylinder, concave shadow—on mornings when I'm tired these notions of mine get me going, they stimulate me, I soon forget them once I start using my eyes."[22] In his work, structure returns based on a geometry that emphasizes the picture plane and inhibits the impulse to look through it to an illusory third dimension. He skews and tilts perspective, filling a shallow space of the picture with faceted forms of equal density, and so prepares the way for Cubism. He proclaims his desire to make paintings that are "a piece of nature." His goal is to paint pictures of things—Mont Sainte-Victoire, a basket of apples—that have the solidity of the thing themselves. Because of its concreteness, his art moves toward abstraction. Things in nature—rocks, driftwood, puddles left by a rainstorm—are "abstract," in that they are not representations of anything else, but "concrete" in that they are completely what they are. And nothing else.

Art is moving with increasing rapidity toward a fork in the road after which the world as it is for me, and as it is without me, in itself, diverge from each other. Art that endeavors to represent the world as it is and as it appears requires those two roads to converge. As the distance between them increases, art that preserves the illusion of representation loses its credibility.

The world may still be represented, but it is represented more in the manner that signs on the doors of lavatories represent men and women than in the way Leonardo represented the *Mona Lisa* or Joshua Reynolds the society ladies and gentlemen whose portraits he painted.

Joshua Reynolds, *Portraits of Lady Worsley and Lord Middleton* (1776, 1762)

Both the bathroom signs and the Reynolds portraits have characteristics by which we recognize them as portraying people. In both a mass on the top, which we read as a head, sits on a narrow column (the neck) that connects to a larger mass (the body) with two symmetrical extensions (the body and arms). Neither the bathroom signs nor the portraits would be mistaken for actual walking, breathing human beings. Human beings are not two-dimensional, static and small enough to fit on a bathroom door or in the frame of the picture. But there is a qualitative difference in the degree to which the bathroom signs and the Reynolds portraits look like people we might bump into on the street. The signs are intentionally generic; the portraits, individualized. The designer of the signs does not fight the flatness of the picture frame; the portrait painter strives for the illusion of three dimensions. We say that the bathroom sign is more "abstract," but it is also more concrete—it is what it is. It does not foster an illusion. When we look at signs on bathroom doors and compare them to examples of 18th century English portraiture there is no question which are the most contemporary, "advanced," and modern. Art is moving in the direction of the bathroom signs.

The canvas has always been a realm apart, but within that separate realm the artist strove to capture the world. Now artists let the world go. Paradoxically, this "letting go" allows them to achieve a new objectivity. The painting is what it is—it is not an illusory representation of something it is not. As part of the letting go, forms become more flexible. Signs pull away from what they signify. So nothing is easier than to take her:

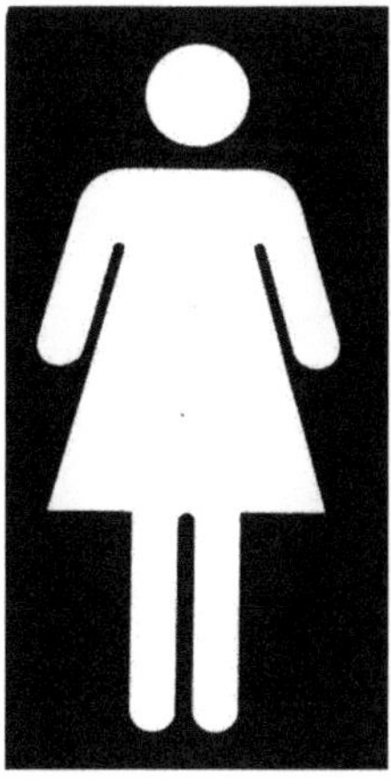

and make her a bit more interesting:

Her kinship to Matisse's late paper cutouts should be self-evident.

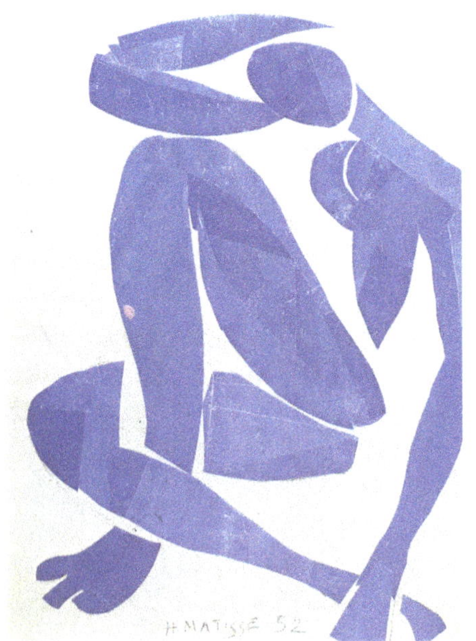

Henri Matisse, *Blue Nude IV* (1952)

I did not feel I was violating the integrity of a woman's body when I cut up and rearranged the figure on the bathroom sign. I feel only peacefulness in the presence of Matisse's *Blue Nude,* though the shapes out of which she is assembled are twisted, elongated, and attached to the body in ways that are anatomically implausible. I could not, however, have cut up the Reynolds portraits or distorted their anatomy without some sense that I was doing violence to the persons he depicted—killing them symbolically, just as my students "killed" the *Mona Lisa* in the process of cutting her to pieces.

A mere 150 years or so separates the Reynolds portraits from Matisse's *Blue Nude IV,* and yet they seem to belong to different worlds. It would be hard to convince an anthropologist from another planet that the tribe that produced the Reynolds had any cultural connection to the tribe that produced the Matisse.

Nevertheless, the Matisse and the Reynolds obey a fundamental convention of pictorial representation—in both there is a boundary between the object and the space surrounding it. The differentiation is less pronounced in the Reynolds. Light, filtered by the atmosphere, reveals form but softens edges. In the bathroom sign and the Matisse the absence of atmosphere and clutter in the background emphasizes the figure/ground distinction. The sign is easy to read from a distance as we rush down the corridor urgently looking for a bathroom.

The bathroom sign has a clear representational function. Its utility depends upon it. But the formal freedom that allows the extreme simplification of the sign also makes possible a complete rejection of the last residues of painting's bondage to representation: the requirement to separate figure from ground; the requirement that the object be distinguishable from the space surrounding it; and finally the requirement of a uniform space, without breaks and dislocations.

Since my reproduction of a bathroom sign serves no purpose, I am free to snip away at it, till it ceases to be recognizable as "woman" and "man" or anything at all.

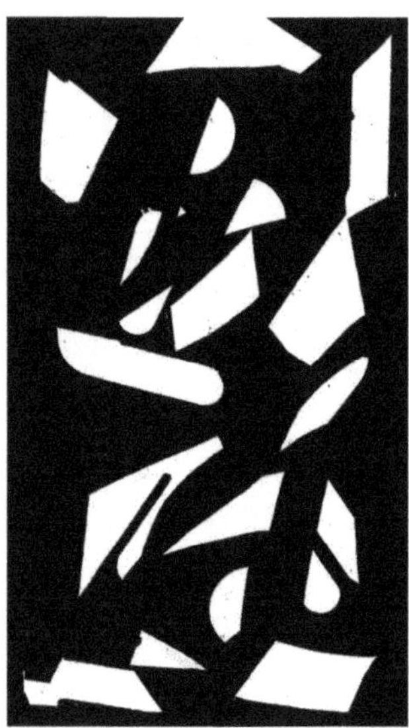

I have arrived at a point that Picasso reached more than 30 years before Matisse's paper cutout: Cubism. My students were the heirs of the Cubists when they dutifully followed my instructions to take scissors to their postcards of the Mona Lisa. In Cubist paintings and collages not only are images sliced and dicecd, but the space the figure inhabits is itself broken into fragments. The figure ceases to be distinguishable from the ground.

Picasso's *Ma Jolie (Woman with a Zither or Guitar)* is for all intents and purposes "nonrepresentational." Whoever gave the painting its title, apparently had reason to believe it contained a reference to a musical instrument, but couldn't decide which. That, however is the least of the uncertainties that would confront us if the painting had no title at all. How could we decide whether what remains in the rubble of representation is a man or a woman (or a tree or a tower)? Were it not for the fact that the forms seems to come to a point toward one of the two shorter sides and "MA JOLIE" is painted in black letters on the bottom, we would not be sure which side is up.

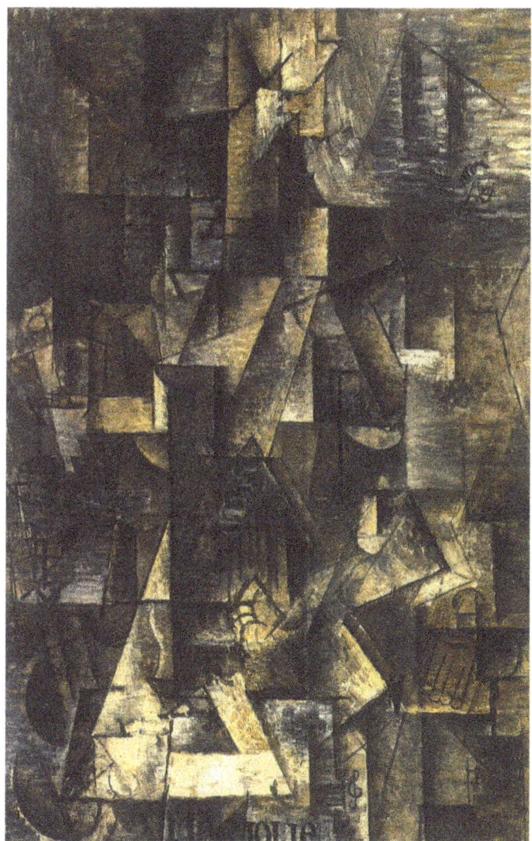

Pablo Picasso, *Ma Jolie (Woman with a Zither or Guitar)* (1911–1912)

Art has reached the cliff of nonrepresentation. Henceforward it will teeter on its edge, sometimes leaping over it, sometimes pulling back. But the easy assumption of representation can no longer be revived. The painting as object stands in the world, free to be whatever it wishes to be.

And so begins a pell-mell rush toward the cacophony of modernism, which starts in Paris, then crosses the Atlantic to New York. In the wake of that stampede, every assumption about what art must be and do is jettisoned like excess baggage abandoned by refugees fleeing a disaster. Every assumption, that is, except that the duty of the artist is to join the triumphal procession led by, first the European, and then the American avant-garde toward . . . god knows where.

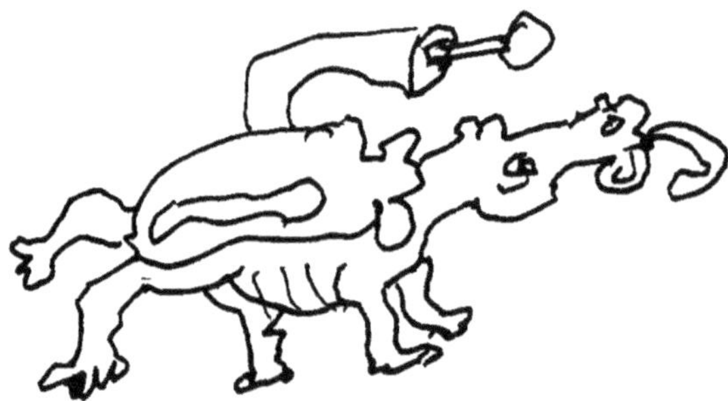

A Bathroom Sign Leads to an Intuition about the Social History of Art

HOW DID IT come to this—the wreckage of all convention, the cacophony of modernism and postmodernism? When did the unraveling begin? And why? The questions are unanswerable if we look at the history of art in isolation. To even begin to craft an answer, we would need a social history of art that would carefully correlate—to use the old Marxist cliché—the "superstructure" of artistic form with the "base" in the material relations of people's actual lives.

Overwhelmed by the enormity of such a task, I have the urge to go to the bathroom.

And there it is before me. The sign for the men's. How clean it is! How devoid of any suggestion of odors, feces, streams of urine, and naked bottoms. In the millennia before flush toilets, all the waste products of the human body could not be concealed so easily. The sign is streamlined; as it conceals waste, so nothing in its form is wasted; it has the sleekness of a race car. It was molded by a machine and appears untouched by human hands.

The bathroom sign is not fine art. It's a tool for directing the flow of human traffic. It marks the location of a door that leads to an inner sanctum where a universal human need can be met. For the greater part of human history images have been tools. Like the bathroom sign, they pointed to a realm that has been set apart. They were a technology of the sacred, valued for their usefulness in communicating with gods and spirits. Form in the service of function reached toward that which lay beyond perception. In hindsight, after centuries of art absorbed in the depiction of eyebrows, dimples, and the shine on the skin of an apple, this art sometimes seems surprisingly contemporary—closer to the bathroom sign than to the Reynolds portraits.

The art created in the West between the Renaissance and the modernism of the 20th century sought the universal in the particular. When Vermeer paints a woman playing the lute, illuminated by light streaming in through the casement of a nearby window, he reveals something essentially human in *this* lute player, seen in *this* light, at *this* moment. The bathroom sign bypasses appearances. It achieves universality by avoiding the particular. Ir represents no actual body—fat or thin, old or young, plain or handsome. It is an icon of modernity, but, carved in wood or stone and dug from the earth, it might be the product some previously unknown tribe not unlike, for example, the Senufo of Côte d'Ivoire.

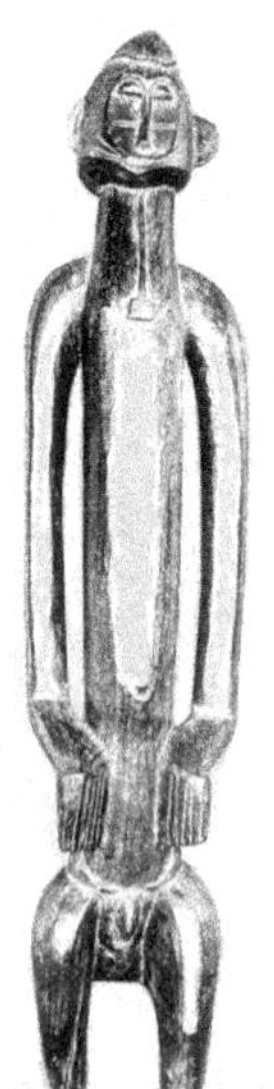

Senufo wood figure

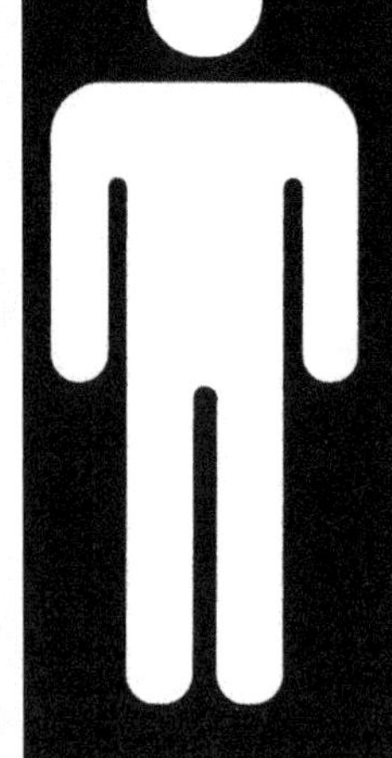

International mens

The similarity, however, is misleading. Images that functioned in the service of magic and religion sought to reveal the awesome supernatural that lay behind and beyond the world of appearances. There is no hint of a beyond in the bathroom sign. Its universality is generic. The figures on bathroom signs represent the common denominator of man and woman, just as money represents the common denominator of all value.

The bathroom sign on the men's was manufactured by a machine in a factory, owned by a corporation that functioned in a global system of competing and sometimes cooperating corporations. In its form—so clean, so plastic, so precise in its geometry—the bathroom sign speaks of the technology by which it is produced and the system of exchange that makes it worthwhile for corporations to mobilize the technology to produce bathroom signs in the multimillions.

In small letters on my bathroom sign is written, "Made in China." Multiple exchanges of money connect me to the Chinese factory that churned out my bathroom sign and to the people who work in that factory. I imagine a young Chinese woman, whose days are spent indentured to a bathroom sign making machine. I do not know her and she does not know me. I cannot sense her presence in this bland plastic rectangle. Whatever her mind was doing—mumbling to itself in Chinese, fleeing and returning to the present—has left no trace. The object is sanitized of all the burbling, boiling incoherence of her thoughts and feelings. She does not contaminate with her touch the plastic rectangle spit out by the machine that she tends. She confronts the job, the factory, the corporation, the system of corporations, the laws that facilitate the corporations as things outside and beyond her control. Her bosses like it that way. Machines function best with the minimum of friction, and the entire economy works best when the mind of the worker is relegated to a sphere of privacy, an internal sphere that poses no danger to the workplace.

The system that connects me to that Chinese woman is also the system that disconnects her from the task that she is doing and the product of her labor. As the world is increasingly integrated by global capitalism, intimate connections between people and things are broken. Capitalism fragments what once was whole and builds a new whole out of the fragments; the circle is broken and rebuilt, but the parts within that circle are divided from each other as they are connected through the medium of money. Just as humanity's collective power over nature increases, individual humans find themselves increasingly powerless. The worker is a divided being, divided within herself and divided from the things that she makes. The power of ownership, the power of the technology, the power of *the system* are not her power. They stand against her.

Our lives are shaped by a system—global, corporate, insatiable, addicted to speed, obeying an imperative to expand or die. As it shapes our lives, so it shapes objects that surround us and our relations to those objects. The bathroom sign and the life of the Chinese worker both bear the imprint of the machine and of the multinational corporation that owns the machine and of the economic system whose imperatives the multinational corporation obeys. The system shapes the life of the Chinese worker. It shapes the life of the CEO who heads the corporation for which the Chinese worker works and the life of the homeless man the CEO steps over at the end of the day as he heads for the parking garage. Necessity imposed by the system shapes our lives and determines the degree of freedom we experience. The CEO has more control over his surroundings than the worker in his factory, but if he steps out of line he will be fired. The homeless man does not have to keep up appearances, but his options for where to sleep are limited. And what of the artist in the modern world? Art serves no function, and therefore remains a realm of freedom within the realm of necessity. And yet, that freedom is not unlimited. What can be done within that realm depends on what is true about the times. Art may be a realm of let's pretend, but only certain pretenses are possible. It is, as the saying goes, "a lie that tells the truth." All that we are, and likewise our relation to all that we are not, is implicated in the making of a work of art. Just as the work of art gives us the universal in the particular, so the work itself is a particular that discloses a universal. In art we sense something that may be at the common core of all those relations that are described in the language of economics, politics, and philosophy—a way of being in the world.

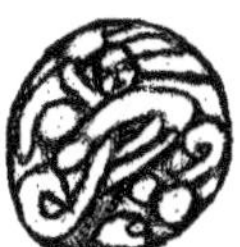

There was a time when people lived in thatched cottages on country lanes and in towns with narrow cobbled streets where horses clomped and sewage ran in the gutters.

Always nearby lay fields and forests. When the sun set and night closed in, candles were lit. People labored in the fields and in workshops near their homes. Many of the things they needed they made themselves. The simple tools they used only came to life when picked up from the workbench. They took the goods they made for trade to the market and sold them to people who needed them. From that world, by a series of steps, some slow, some sudden, we reach the world of the bathroom sign, modern art, the Chinese worker, and ourselves. In the rush of change that is the history of the West, the bourgeoisie rose to power and accumulated wealth. Advances in technology and war allowed super exploitation of people and nature. Eventually the tentacles of capital reached to every corner of the globe.

The rush of change in all the outward and material circumstances of people's lives has been accompanied—how could it have been otherwise?—by inward and invisible changes in people's sense of self and their relation to the world. Human beings have always had a sense of self; self consciousness is a universal component of the all-human consciousness. But the extent to which we are *conscious* of our self-consciousness, the extent to which it becomes the focus of attention, is unlikely to have been a constant and more likely to have evolved over time. A change in self-consciousness necessarily involves a change in consciousness of the world. Increasing consciousness of self—of being a world within a world—brings with it the potential of discord between the self and the world. The world as it is and as it is reflected in consciousness may not be the same; appearances may not reflect reality.

For millennia a person's place in society was determined by heredity. No amount of effort could change a serf into a lord, or convert a member of one tribe into that of another. Each "I" was only an aspect of a "we." The past ruled over the present in the form of tradition. In the course of the historical changes that bring us from tradition-bound societies to the present in which capitalism mandates that all things must change or die, the "I" individuates; an autonomous self frees itself from the "we" to confront all that is "not-I" from a distance and without attachment. The individual is freed to master people and to make a name for himself (usually not "herself"). A self that is self-aware confronts the world to which it is not bound—the world as object—which is there to be pounded, pulverized, dissolved, and dissected till it gives up its secrets and succumbs to its human master. The object, shorn of connection to the self, falls into the domain of science, which prides itself on an objectivity, which it obtains by excluding any trace of subjectivity. From science is born powerful technologies that make possible the exploitation of nature on an unprecedented scale and the conquest of peoples whose technology is at a lower level. Vast wealth is accumulated, control of which is ultimately seized by the bourgeoisie, which becomes the dominant class, displacing an aristocracy of lords and ladies, kings and princes, not a few of whom end up beneath the blade of guillotine. With the coming of the Industrial Revolution, the power of technology increases exponentially. The bourgeoisie reigns supreme; beneath it a new class forms, the proletariat.

In the *Communist Manifesto,* Marx and Engels marveled at the pace and scale of the transformation wrought by the bourgeoisie:

> The bourgeoisie cannot exist without constantly revolutionizing the instruments of production, and thereby the relations of production, and with them the whole relations of society. Conservation of the old modes of production in unaltered form was, on the contrary, the first condition of existence for all earlier industrial classes. Constant revolutionizing of production, uninterrupted disturbance of all social conditions, everlasting uncertainty and agitation distinguish the bourgeois epoch from all earlier ones. All fixed, fast-frozen relations, with their train of ancient and venerable prejudices and opinions, are swept away, all new-formed ones become antiquated before they can ossify. All that is solid melts into air, all that is holy is profaned, and man is at last compelled to face with sober senses his real conditions of life, and his relations with his kind.

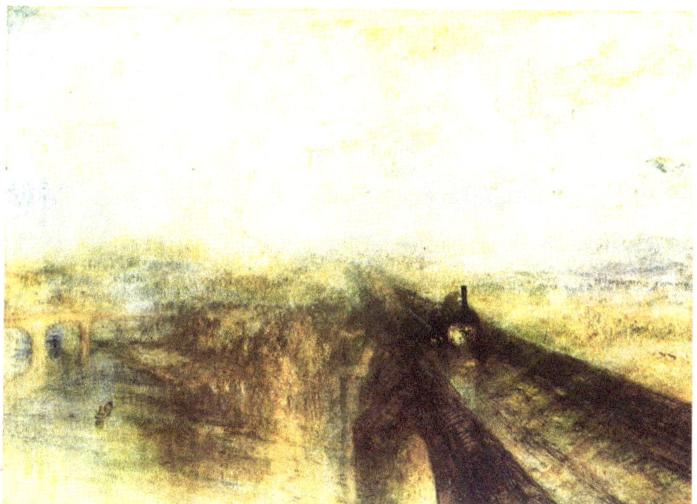

J. M. W. Turner, *Rain Steam and Speed—the Great Western Railway* (1844)

"All that is solid melts into air"! The *Manifesto* was published in 1848. Four years earlier, J. M. W. Turner first exhibited *Rain Steam and Speed—the Great Western Railway* in which nothing remains of the locomotive, the tracks, and solid earth but swirling emanations. All "fast-frozen relations" have disappeared. Forty-eight years after Turner painted *The Great Western*, Monet, who admired and studied Turner, caused the Rouen Cathedral to melt into a kaleidoscope of light. For both artists, change is the only constant and the energy of light takes precedence over the solidity of matter. [23]

Turner and Monet paint in the times of which the *Communist Manifesto* speaks. Trains move at unprecedented speed; machinery pounds away at an ever accelerating pace; soon steam will be replaced by electricity, providing light that blasts away the darkness of night—these revolutions in the means of production are accompanied by revolutions in thought that sweep away all "venerable prejudices and opinions."

Marx and Engels expressed the belief—the hope—that when all those prejudices and holy mystifications were swept away we would be compelled to face "the real conditions of our lives." It has not been the case. New mystifications constantly spring up to replace the old. But the real remains, though continually obscured. The Great Western Railway lost in clouds of steam and swirling atmospherics and the Rouen Cathedral changing moment by moment as the light changes in Monet's series of paintings, do not, in fact, disappear. The train will run you over if you wander onto its tracks, and a stone dislodged from the Cathedral will crush you if you are unlucky enough to be standing beneath it when it falls. The estrangement of the Impressionists from the object world of mass and solidity reflects not only the times and the revolutions in technology, but also the estrangement of the bourgeois, whose comfortable lives they chronicled, from the proletariat whose muscles ached from lifting and hauling heavy objects.

The hard and impregnable things which find no place in Impressionism weigh down on the Chinese worker in the bathroom sign factory. Her thoughts drift away from the noise and endless repetitive motions of the factory. They can find no purchase in the products of her labor nor the means of their production. The energy that runs the machinery she operates is not her energy. The Impressionists could make of their impressions something solid—a painted rectangle of canvas—a transitional object between the self and the world. She has no such ability. Art may no longer have that ability. The system, which has produced technologies that split the atom, split the self from the world in new and unprecedented ways. Separated from the world, the self splinters; the object becomes its enemy.

> The object which labor produces—labor's product—confronts it as *something alien*, as a *power independent* of the producer. The product of labor is labor which has been congealed in an object, which has become material: it is the *objectification* of labor. Labor's realization is its objectification. In the conditions dealt with by political economy this realization of labor appears as loss of reality for the workers; objectification as *loss of the object* and *object-bondage*; appropriation as *estrangement*, as *alienation*.
>
> So much does labor's realization appear as loss of reality that the worker loses reality to the point of starving to death. So much does objectification appear as loss of the object that the worker is robbed of the objects most necessary not only for his life but for his work. [24]

Loss of the object. Estrangement. Alienation. What Marx foresaw for the worker, perhaps is the fate of all of us. The bourgeoisie itself is infected; the forces it unleashed are destroying it. In Renaissance Italy, the discovery of perspective placed the artist's eye in the center of the world. Around that center, the world was ordered and organized. Now the center does not hold. We can no longer make a true picture of the world by drawing a circle with ourselves as the compass point. Art veers between poles of subject and object, just as the attention of the worker in the toilet sign factory veers between her dreams and her reality. We have art that is all sensibility and self-expression; and we have art that treats all subjectivity as smog, obscuring our view of the object. We have bathroom signs with no soul, and souls wandering the planet looking for a home.

Things fall apart. Things have been falling apart for some time. The real becomes less so and art stumbles toward its future.*

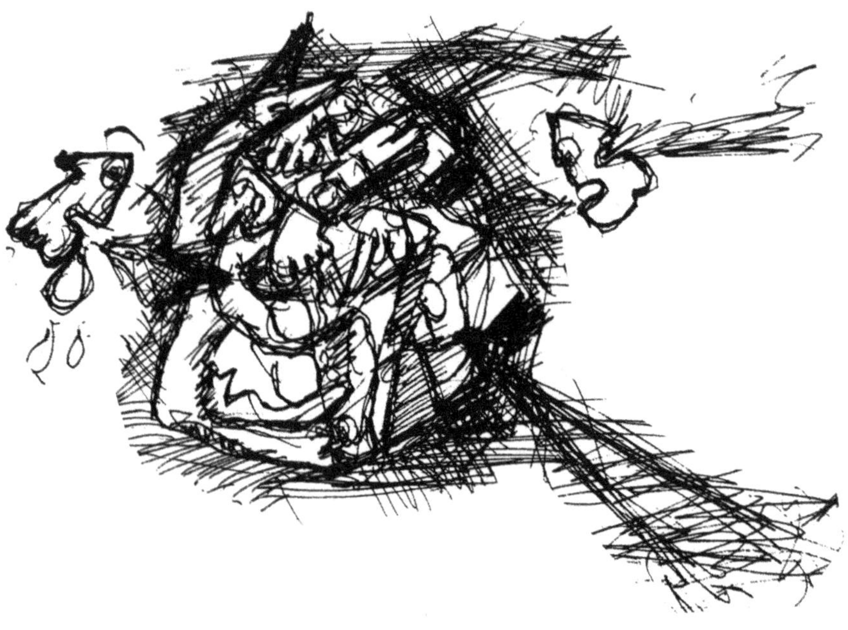

* As there are new forms of alienation in the modern world, so there are new forms of integration. Consciousness, left to itself, is a dangerous sphere from which potential opposition could grow. The worker may be divided from other workers, she may find the objects that are the product of her labor cold, alien, and opaque; insofar as she is present at work, she may be divided from herself. But as a consumer she is integrated into the system; she confronts objects that appeal to her; speak to her, seduce her; she see herself reflected in them. As the world is fragmented, it is at the same time subject to a totalitarian integration that no previous world has ever experienced. Art that reflects alienation and estrangement of a self splintered from the world may be seen as a protest against a totalitarianism that proclaims us all one big happy family. The worker can protest by breaking her machine, or climbing to the roof of the factory and throwing herself to her death. Art protests by breaking into pieces and flirting with suicide.

I Paint. I Stop. I Discover Mural Painting and Start Again.

IN 1962, I thought I might be the future of art. That was the year I had dropped out of graduate school at Yale and moved to the Lower East Side of New York, determined to become a painter. I rented a cheap railroad apartment. The toilet was in a closet; the bathtub was in the kitchen next to the sink. It had an enameled tin cover that served as a dinner table and desk. I spent hours that stretched into days and months painting the sink and the bathtub, and occasionally the toilet. I was fascinated by the way perspective lines translated into geometric shapes on the surface of the canvas. I ignored the rust on the pipes, the chips in the enamel, and the skuzzy film of filth on the linoleum. My life was in chaos, but my paintings were precise and meticulous. I relished the irony that I, whose childhood had been consumed in battles with my mother about cleanliness and my inability to keep my room tidy, was choosing to paint the plumbing.

I was aware that my narrow choice of subject matter was entirely arbitrary and equally aware that if I tried to go beyond it I would be lost. *All* limits were arbitrary. There was no reason to paint one way rather than another. I was earning a little money writing capsule art reviews for *Art News Magazine.* Abstract Expressionism no longer reigned supreme in the uptown galleries I visited. The art world was fragmenting, and all the fragments were circling in orbits that bypassed the little way station on the Lower East Side where I was conducting my experiments in representation.

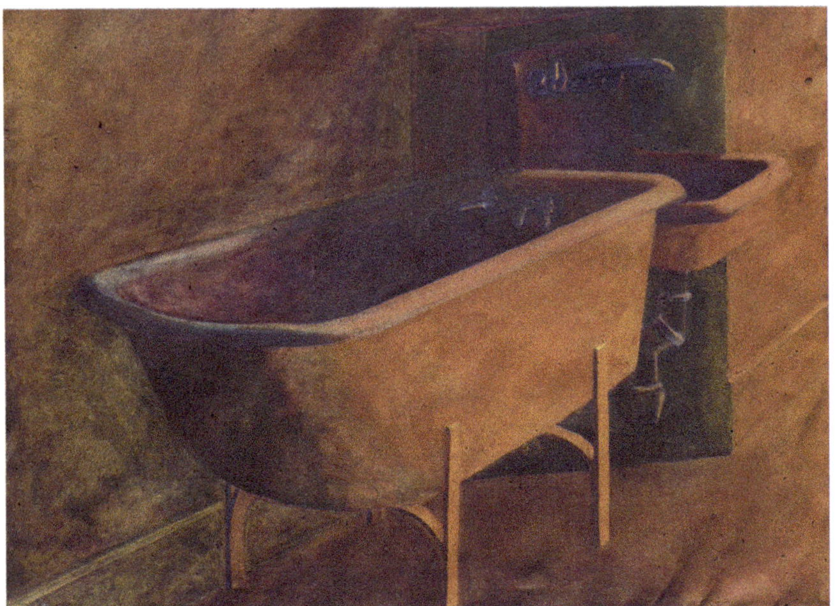

Osha Neumann, *Bathtub* (1960)

Undeterred I kept on painting bathtubs. There was still something there that I needed to explore. And then one day, there wasn't. The plumbing ceased to matter. I no longer looked at it with rapt attention; I was no longer willing to dutifully follow its outlines as if it were my master and I its slave. I was like someone who had been terribly in love and wakes up one day feeling nothing for the person he had previously adored. My special relationship to my sink and my bathtub came to end like a marriage gone sour.

In my last bathtub painting, my brushwork became more violent; drab local color went up in flames, and the neat uncluttered geometry of my previous paintings was disrupted by a photograph torn from the newspaper that I painted as if it were lying on the floor under the tub. It depicted a tank dragging the half naked corpse of a Vietnamese man along the ground by two ropes tied to his feet. An American soldier, riding on top of the tank looks back at the body with the nonchalance of a truck driver checking to make sure a trailer is securely hitched.

With that painting, the floodgates opened.

I went from painting meticulous geometric canvasses to creating wall-sized assemblages of women's undergarments, pee-stained mattresses, old shoes, cigarette butts, mutilated dolls, crushed cans and broken bottles—whatever rank fetid, scabrous, rotting offal I could find in my wanderings through Lower East Side streets—all of which I glued together with melted wax. It was as if all the plumbing in my earlier canvases had backed up and overflowed onto the walls of my apartment. Once I gave a friend of mine one of my smaller works featuring an old boot. He hung it over his bed and awoke one night to find a line of cockroaches, descending from their hideout in the boot toward his pillow.

I could paint my bathtub series as long as something was at stake. That "something" was no small matter. All my relations—to things, to myself, to others—were implicated in my relation to that nondescript inconsequential piece of enameled metal. If I could master that relationship, I felt that the great ocean liner of the world would change course, with the painting at the helm. New possibilities would be revealed, old truths renewed.

Every painting was a gamble. Could I make of my being there with the bathtub, viewing it from where I was standing in front of my easel at that particular hour on that particular day something that could resist the passage of time? Could I create paintings that would be islands of meaningful order amidst the emotional and physical chaos of my life? The answer for a while was "Yes." And then it was "No."

The spatial relations between the fixtures in my kitchen, determined by nothing more profound than the limited budget of a cheap-ass landlord, ceased to have any meaning for me. I lost interest in studying the lines of perspective out of which I had constructed the geometry of my canvases. I had created my little islands of order by excluding whatever would disturb their peace and tranquility. Now all that I had excluded demanded reentry. I'd concealed the violence of my emotions in careful brushwork. I'd denied my tormented sadomasochistic sexual fantasy life in my choice of form and subject matter. I'd painted naked plumbing rather than naked women. And I'd excluded all the disorder, chaos, and filth of the ghetto, which, thanks to my mother's constant scolding, I'd come to believe was the perfect visible expression of my own disordered, chaotic, and filthy mind.

I could no longer hide from myself in the clean, well-lighted universe of my plumbing paintings. In creating the scabrous assemblages to which I now devoted all my energy, I gave vent to the emotional ferocity I had been keeping firmly in check. I reveled in the ugliness and filth of my materials, accepting them into my life as a born-again Christian accepts Christ. Filth would be my redemption. On the other side of all the chaos, I sought a new order, a new beauty, and a new necessity of forms. But I did not find it. There was no stopping point, no place where the urge to rip and rend and confess would ever be satisfied, no order I could create that I could believe in.

I had reached a place to which most artists arrive at some point in their career. Paintings labored on for days cannot be made to work and are painted over. Drawings for which they had high hopes are crumpled and thrown in the wastebasket. The dream of being a great undiscovered artist turns into a nightmare of certain failure. When they reach this juncture some artists keep struggling and achieve a breakthrough. Others give up and decide they're better suited for a different profession.

I did not persevere in my search for a Northwest Passage through my difficulties. I no longer believed in the purpose of the journey. In my visits to uptown galleries I had seen nothing compelling, nothing that did not seem arbitrary and capricious, nothing that convincingly made a case for itself. I knew my limitations, but I convinced myself that the limits against which I battered were the limits of art itself.

Art was sick and was unlikely to recover. I began writing an essay that I intended to be my farewell to art. Art, I wrote, had lost its way;

it was always pushing against limits, but in refusing every limitation, it was committing suicide, because all art depends on limitation to maintain itself against the formlessness of life. And while art was committing suicide in the posh uptown galleries of midtown Manhattan, a cultural revolution was ripping children from their families, and depositing them, long-haired and stoned, on the sidewalks of the Lower East Side. The '60s were in full swing. The winds of revolution were trembling the pedestals of power.

"All power to the imagination," shouted the rebellious students of the Sorbonne in May 1968. The time had come for the imagination to leave the prison of art and take command of life. The goal of revolution was the total imaginative transformation of the world. "Be realistic, demand the impossible," another of their slogans, was a call to fight for the fulfillment of our most utopian dreams, Heretofore those dreams could only find expression in poetry and song. Now they became the program of the revolution. It was no longer possible to stand aside. All hands were required on deck. I left the manuscript of my essay unfinished and became a Motherfucker.

For a few short years I swam in the roiling riptide of the '60s. I ran with my little anarchist street gang, made a few crude drawings for our flyers, and never looked back with any sense of loss to my days as an artist. And when the riptide of the '60s, having dragged me out to sea, reversed, and tossed me up on the dry shores of a world that we had not succeeded in remaking, I could not imagine going back to painting—until I saw the murals that Chicano artists were painting on the walls of the Mission District of San Francisco.

Here was a way around art's dead end. It was not necessary to follow the avant-garde over the cliff into anti-art. The line of march could be reversed. Art did not need to be a private affair. You could do it in the street. Isolated in my Lower East side apartment, I had lost faith that art could still fulfill its mission of bridging the gulf between the self and the

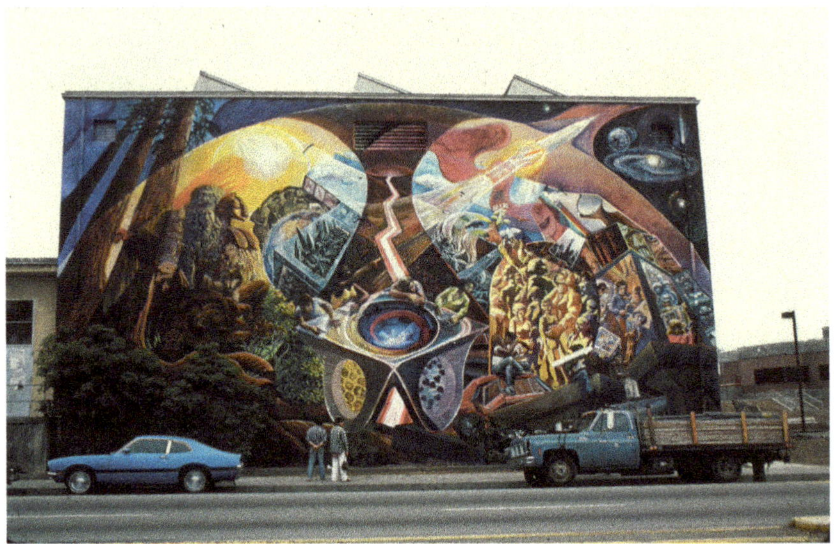

Osha Neumann, O'Brian Thiele, Daniel Galvez, *Intersections,* Willard Jr. High School (1980)

world. The gulf was too wide. But now I saw that, embedded in community and performed in public, art could resist its dissolution. It could be renewed; the center could hold. On common ground, a foundation could be built for a new beginning.

I decided to turn myself into a muralist. My first efforts were pathetic. I contributed an embarrassingly bad mural to the kiddy corral of the welfare center where I went to collect my food stamps. I couldn't draw people—a terrible flaw in a mural painter. They came out bulbous and boneless. I took classes in anatomy and improved somewhat, but try as I might, I could never remember how arms worked, how the biceps changed shape when the arm was flexed, where the triceps fit, how the ulna and the radius crossed and uncrossed depending on whether the hand was palm up or palm down. I did my best to fake it. When I was working on a mural, I would take my various anatomy books with me and thumb through them trying to find an illustration of a limb in a position that resembled the one I was trying to paint. I had a similar problem with folds of clothing. Well done, they can be formal miracles, the visual equivalent of music. My folds hung, flaccid and unconvincing, on the somewhat arbitrary anatomy of my figures.My strength lay in design. A mural is like an iceberg. The greater part of the work that goes into it happens before you set up your scaffold on the street.

You cannot just go up to a wall thirty feet high and fifty feet wide and start painting. You need to work out your ideas in a drawing whose dimensions are proportional to the wall, an inch to a foot or some other manageable ratio. You have to consider the point of view of the spectator. If you cut off figures at the bottom of the mural, they will appear to be rising up out of the sidewalk. Time spent on small details at the top will be wasted because they'll disappear at a distance. If you want to tell a complex story with multiple figures, you may have to tilt the perspective, so that people are not all packed in on a single level, peering over each other's shoulders. If there is a window or door in a wall, you have to take that into consideration. You need an overall rhythm that carries from one end of the mural to the other and unifies the composition. And if you're using symbols or metaphors, they have to be comprehensible.

I enjoyed the intellectual challenge of solving the compositional and thematic problems of mural design. In some of my projects I was the sole designer; in others a group of painters worked out the design collectively. The painting of the mural was always a group effort. I was lucky in finding artists to work alongside me, cover up my mistakes, and bring to life the rudimentary figures I'd drawn in my cartoon for the mural.

I loved everything about painting murals. I loved the banter with passersby. I loved clambering up and down scaffolding. I loved running across the street, heedless of the traffic, in order to judge whether what I'd just painted was comprehensible from a distance. I loved painting big—big hands, big faces, big everything. I loved working with other painters, standing with them during a break, admiring a particularly well painted passage that one of us had executed. I loved that we were putting subversive content in a public space dominated by billboards. I loved the appreciation we received for doing it. I felt I'd stumbled on a way to combine art and politics that enhanced both.

In every way, mural painting was the opposite of the solipsistic struggles of the studio artist. It was a public celebration of the communal spirit. We had no interest in or contact with the "art world" of galleries and critics. The whole cultural apparatus that anointed trendsetters and determined the value of a work of art in the market ignored us and we ignored it.

Until I discovered mural painting, I was convinced that the economic and political hegemony of Europe and the United States implied cultural hegemony. The United States had the most advanced economy, so necessarily it had the most advanced art. In the first part of the 20th century, modern art had no choice but to "progress" in the direction taken by art movements that were centered in Paris. In the latter half of the century, the center moved to New York. I had come to the conclusion that "progress" led inevitably to a cul-de-sac. Avant-garde artists had shattered the flattering mirror that art had once held up to the world. It was not possible to piece it back together. Since most people still like pretty pictures of an easily recognizable world with no loose ends dangling, they would necessarily dismiss avant-garde art as obscure and unintelligible. A small urban elite would continue to attend gallery openings and subscribe to *Art News*, but the unenlightened majority would pursue more accessible pleasures. If I didn't follow the lead of the avant-garde and continue to paint in a style that was past its pull date, my art would be irrelevant and aesthetically reactionary. If I didn't like where art was heading I could stop making art and find some other way to occupy my time.

I now realized I had been wrong. There was a way to avoid the trap. The story of art had more than one plot line. I discovered the great Mexican muralists, *Los Tres Grandes*, Diego Rivera, José Clemente Orozco, and David Alfaro Siqueiros. I had not learned about them in

Swarthmore and I had not taught them in my art history class, but they had produced some of the greatest paintings of the 20th century.

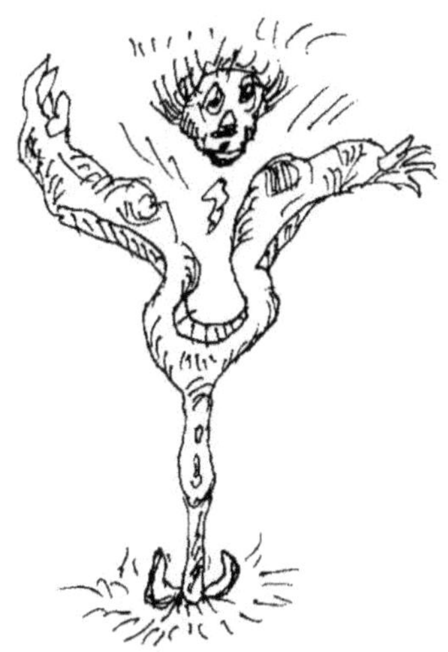

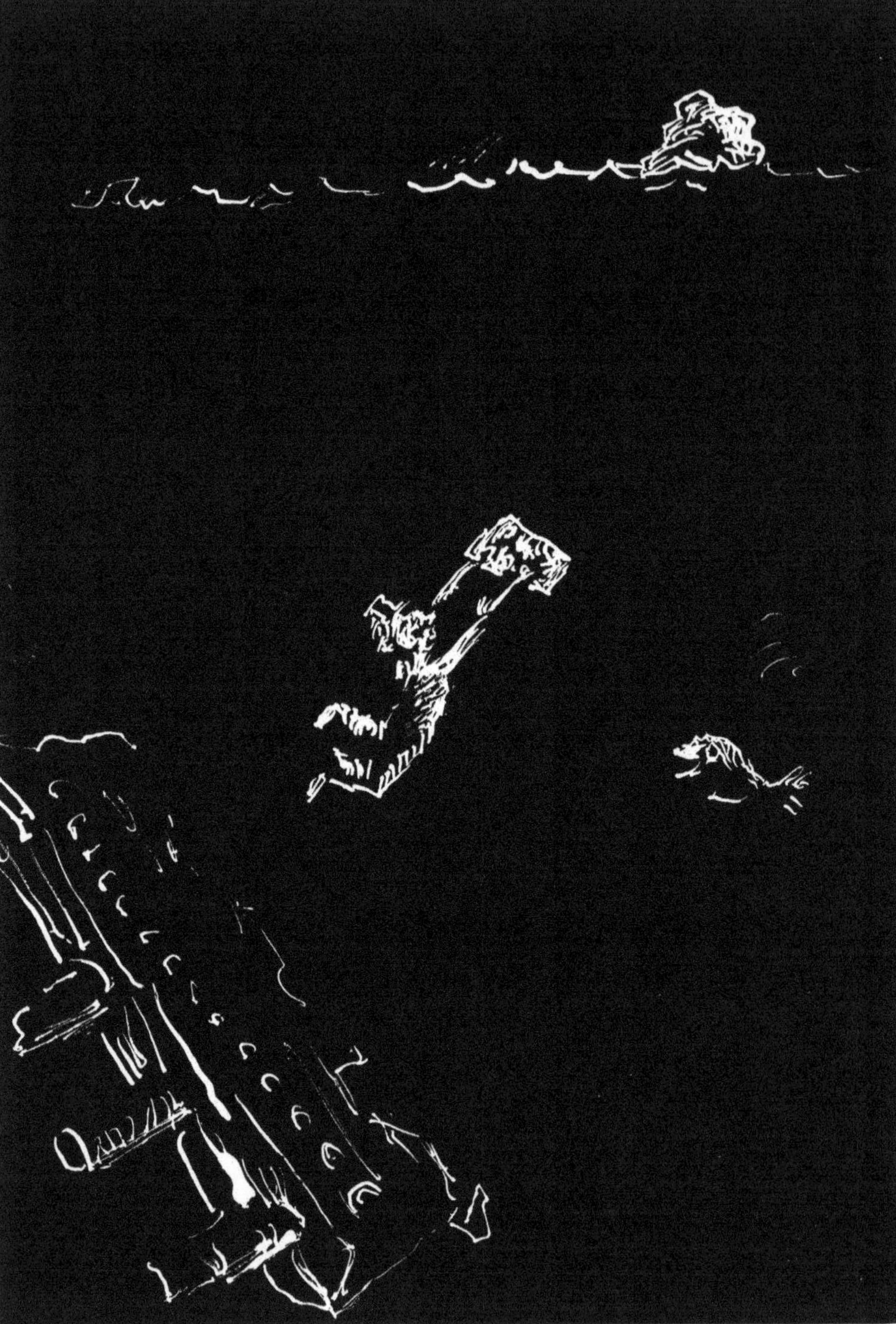

Los Tres Grandes

THERE IS NO recipe for producing great art. There are no set of historical circumstances that make it inevitable. But something had happened in Mexico that drew the artist and his world together and made a great synthetic art possible. That something was the Mexican Revolution. Mexico was in a process of sloughing off political and cultural dependence on Europe and forging its own unique mestizo identity. It was giving birth to itself in waves of blood and violence. A dizzying torrent of coups and rebellions raised and then dashed hopes for social change. All claims to legitimacy were open to question. No hierarchy went unchallenged. Unrest in the body politic fevered the brains of artists and intellectuals, inspiring them to reinvent themselves with pride as indigenous children of their native land. It was as if the cataracts were suddenly removed that had prevented them from seeing their country, its landscape, its peoples, and its tumultuous history as worthy subjects for representation. Rivera spent the bloody years of the Mexican Revolution in Europe, primarily in Paris, where he experimented with Cubism before abandoning it as being "too fixed and restricted" for what he wanted to say.[25] Returning to Mexico in 1921, he wrote:

> My homecoming produced an esthetic exhilaration which it is impossible to describe. It was as if I were born anew, born into a new world. All the colors I saw appeared to be heightened; they

> were clearer, richer, finer, and more full of light. The dark tones had a depth that they had never had in Europe. I was in the very center of the plastic world, where forms and colors existed in absolute purity. In everything I saw a potential masterpiece—the crowds, the markets, the festivals, the marching battalions, the working men in the shops and fields—in every glowing face, in every luminous child. All was revealed to me. I had the conviction that if I lived a hundred lives I could not exhaust even a fraction of the store of buoyant beauty. [26]

The revolution did more than open the eyes of artists to the beauty of the land. It brought to power governments willing to give them walls to paint. Now all that Rivera had learned in Paris could be put to use populating great expanses of public space with images of his choosing. Monumental art requires structure and clarity. Both Rivera and Siqueiros credit Cézanne with showing them how it was possible to restore the solidity to forms that had been dissolved in the flickering light bath of Impressionism. Rivera learned from Cubism how to fill pictorial space with solids and voids of equal density, a skill that now allowed him to cover great expanses of wall with narrative elements of equivalent importance.

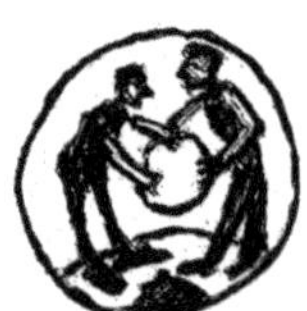

For centuries, European artists stood alone before blank canvases and wrestled to fill them with shapes and colors. Painting was a battle to create a transitional object belonging equally to the boundless world of consciousness and the bounded world of things. It was a private battle. The "I" of the artist, absorbed in the struggle, had only a tangential relationship to a "we." The world waited for the artist to emerge from his solitary battle bearing a work of art. As a cat brings a mouse it has killed and lays it at the feet of its favorite human, so the artist presented his art to the public, hoping for praise and remuneration.

The freedom to engage in the struggle for form, without obligation except to form itself, required that art forego any attempt to intervene directly in the workaday world where only the consciousness of injustice testifies to the possibility of freedom.

In the second half of the 19th century and the beginning of the 20th, artists used their freedom to produce objects that looked nothing like what paintings were supposed to look like. The public expected art to *re-present* the world as stable and comprehensible. Avant-garde art did the opposite. It destabilized and obscured and fragmented. Like the mirror in Snow White, it gave the wrong answer to the question, "Who's the fairest one of all?"

The destabilizing impact of modern art was confined to the domain of cultural values and expectations. No one was sent to the hospital when the edifice of representation collapsed. But the destruction of expectations that art accomplished in the realm of the imagination, the guns, mustard gas, and bayonets of World War I achieved in bloody reality.

Out of the cankerous maw of war, emerged the first nation to declare itself Communist. The leaders of the so-called "free world" trembled that the contagion of revolution would spread from Russia at capitalism's underdeveloped periphery to its core. Communist parties threatened to culture the germ of revolution into a full-blown global epidemic. Catching the fever, artists felt the pull to join the struggle. As *Los Tres Grandes* were climbing scaffolds in Mexico to paint its revolution, André Breton and his fellow surrealists proclaimed their commitment to a program of "absolute nonconformism,"[27] "total revolt,"[28] and "systematic refusal . . . directed . . . against a whole series of intellectual, moral and social obligations that continually and from all sides weighed down on man and crushed him."[29] For weapons they mined the unconscious. Freud was their Virgil, guiding them through the underworld. They emerged with fur-lined tea cups, floating locomotives, and melting watches.

Our cry in the '60s, "All power to the imagination," would have been welcomed by the Surrealists thirty-plus years earlier. Our "Great Refusal" resembled theirs. Like them, we remade the language of politics, fevering its imagery and importing into our manifestoes dreams and drug-fueled fantasies. And like them, we remained isolated from the great mass of suffering humanity, which would need to be mobilized if the total revolution we imagined were ever to succeed.

The Mexican muralists had a connection to a people and its struggle none of the Surrealists could match. They had a story to tell—the story of a nation giving birth to itself. They did not share their Surrealist brethren's fascination with dreams. In dreams all fast-frozen relations unfreeze and recombine improbably. And then you awake, stuck in reality. For *Los Tres Grandes*, to be awake was enough. Awake, they dreamed a nation into existence on the walls of Mexico's buildings.*

It would be too simple to say that because Mexican muralists found a way to return to the people and join their struggle all the tensions between the realms of art and politics were resolved. Politics and art remained uneasy bedfellows. Siqueiros drafted a manifesto in which the artists who had joined his Syndicate of Technical Workers, Painters, and Sculptors proclaimed their commitment to "socialize artistic expression and wipe out bourgeois individualism." They pledged to use "their best

* The Mexican Revolution and the muralists who identified with it were not unaffected by events in Europe. Trotsky, fleeing Stalin's teams of assassins, took refuge in Mexico City where he was befriended by Rivera and Kahlo and survived an assassination attempt led by Siqueiros. Breton visited Trotsky and Rivera and stayed long enough to write, with Trotsky, a manifesto, "For an Independent Revolutionary Art." It was signed by Breton and Rivera, and summed up the relation of art to politics in the slogans:

> "The independence of art—for the revolution."
> "The revolution—for the complete liberation of art."

(André Breton, "Manifesto For an Independent Revolutionary Art" 1938 in *What Is Surrealism: Selected Writings*, ed. Frank Rosemont. New York: Monad Press, 1978, 187).

efforts to produce ideological works of art for the people." They declared that "art must no longer be the expression of individual satisfaction which it is today, but should aim to become a fighting, educative art for all."[30] Both Rivera and Orozco signed the declaration, but in practice neither demonstrated any interest in subordinating their art to the demands of anyone's political agenda.

Rivera's appetite for creation was insatiable. Women, revolutions, the entire history of Mexico and its landscape, the temples of the Aztecs and great auto plants of Detroit—he loved them all and they all become grist for the mill of his artistic imagination. The man who signed his name to a declaration that "art must no longer be the expression of individual satisfaction" looked back on his life and asked himself, "What sort of man was I?" He answered: "I had never had any morals at all and lived only for pleasure where I found it."[31] And Frida Kahlo, who knew him, loved him, and suffered his infidelities, wrote:

> To Diego painting is everything. He prefers his work to anything else in the world. . . . Therefore he cannot lead a normal life. Nor does he ever have the time to think whether what he does is moral, amoral or immoral. . . He has only one great social concern: to raise the standard of living of the Mexican Indians, whom he loved so deeply.[32]

Of the three great ones, Orozco was the clearest in rejecting any political demands upon his art. "I played no part in the Revolution," he writes in his autobiography "I came to no harm, and I ran no danger at all. To me the Revolution was the gayest and most diverting of carnivals."[33] He derided the idea of a political art. "No artist," he said, "has, or ever has had, political convictions of any sort. Those who profess to have them are not artists."[34] As might be expected, he had little patience for those artists who claimed that they were the true revolutionaries, because they painted for the proletariat:

> Proletarian art consisted in pictures of workers on the job, and it was supposedly intended for them. But this turned out to be an error, since a worker who has spent eight hours in the shop takes no pleasure in coming home to a picture of workers on the job. On the other hand the comical thing about it all was that the bourgeois bought proletarian art at fancy prices, though it was supposed to be directed at them, and the proletarians would gladly have bought bourgeois art if they had had the money and, for want of it, found an agreeable substitute in calendar chromos: aristocratic maidens indolently reclining on bearskin rugs or a most elegant looking gentleman kissing a marquise by the light of the moon on a castle terrace.[35]

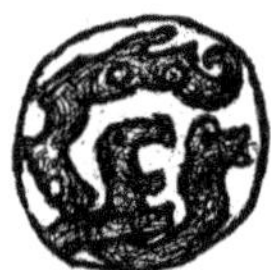

Los Tres Grandes were the inspiration of the community mural movement, whose work I first encountered in my walk through the Mission and to which I was now committed. I did not dwell on the Great One's relationship to the social upheavals of the times, nor on the fact that by the time they set up their scaffolds the most profound revolutionary impulses had been thwarted. Emiliano Zapata had been assassinated, and Francisco "Pancho" Villa had retired from battle, though he too would soon fall victim to assassins' bullets. I did not notice how different our way of working—collectively, with input solicited from the community—was from theirs. They were the yardstick by which I measured our achievement.

We were not the first artists north of the border whom they had inspired. Rivera, Siqueiros, and Orozco had all come to the United States at various points in their careers. Siqueiros came to Los Angeles in 1932 and painted one fresco, *America Tropical*, which depicted a figure with

Indian features, naked, except for a loincloth, bound to a cross on which perched an American eagle.

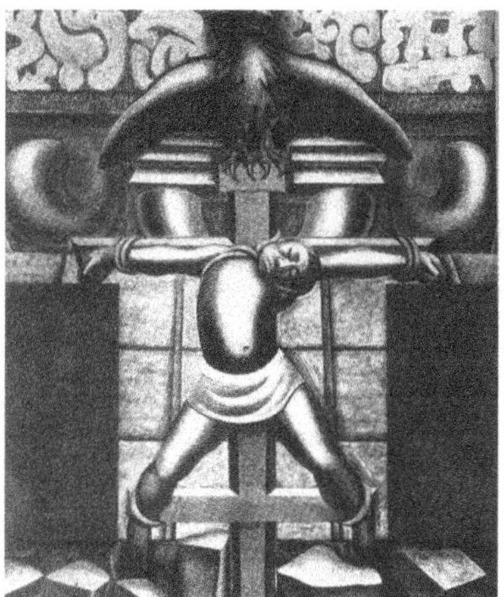

David Alfredo Siqueos, *America Tropical* (detail), 1932

Within six months it was painted over at the instigation of influential members of the downtown Los Angeles business establishment. Siqueiros was deported later that year for political activities. He returned to New York in 1936, where he gave a workshop (attended by Jackson Pollock) with the title "A Laboratory of Modern Techniques in Art." The workshop was affiliated with the Communist Party. Siqueiros encouraged the participants to experiment "with revolutionary materials such as enamel paint and spray guns . . . and at the same time he introduced them to leftist politics."[36] They designed political floats for the Mayday parade of 1936, "which incorporate a revolutionary technique with a radical political content."[37] They experimented with "brushless methods of painting, such as spraying, pouring, and puddling, as well as with different kinds of non-traditional paints, such as industrial paints and silk-screen printing."[38]

Orozco painted severe and implacable murals at the New School for Social Research in New York, Pomona College in California, and—perhaps his most daring work in the United States—the Dartmouth College library. Rivera, an off-again on-again member of the Communist Party, eagerly accepted commissions from the most famous capitalists in America. Edsel Ford (son of Henry) hired him to paint a mural depicting the Rouge assembly plant on the walls of the Detroit Institute of Arts. A month before he arrived, four workers had been killed in a protest at the gates of the plant, but no hint of labor unrest disturbs the rhythm of the assembly line in Rivera's glorious celebration of the productive power of capital. From Detroit, Rivera moved to New York to paint a mural for the Rockefellers on their newly constructed Center. His *Man at the Crossroads* might still be gracing the entranceway of the RCA building had he not insisted on adding a portrait of Lenin—absent from the design he had submitted for approval—thus provoking a confrontation that ultimately resulted in the mural being chipped into piles of multicolored plaster rubble.

It was Rivera, more than either Orozco or Siqueiros, who influenced a generation of social realists, many of whom found employment with the WPA decorating post offices, courthouses, and the stairwells and internal hallways of San Francisco's Coit Tower.

The more I struggled with the demands of mural painting, the more I was awed by Rivera's achievement. I and many of my fellow muralists used his murals as guides in developing our somewhat generic style of collective mural making. But I discovered very quickly, like all the other would be Riveraistas, that I was no Rivera. A mural that fails in the aesthetic dimension of form cannot be redeemed in the realm of morals and politics. A poorly painted, hand, foot, or face will not *be there*, alive, fully present, unique and universal. It doesn't get a free pass if it happens to be the foot of Martin Luther King marching in Selma, or the hand of Harriet Tubman reaching to help a slave to freedom, or the face of Malcolm X speaking on a street corner in Harlem. We could not rely on the radicalism of our content to overcome the weakness of our forms. A poorly painted hand may still be recognizable as a hand, but it will not have a meaning—in itself, as a hand—beyond words and slogans. And if all that is required of a painting is that what it portrays is recognizable, then art has added nothing to politics.

Avant-garde art in Europe had shown that academic conventions of representation were a lie, but had not replaced those conventions with credible new forms of representation. I believed that *Los Tres Grandes* had succeeded where the modern art of Europe had failed. But increasingly, I came to feel that we had failed to follow in their footsteps.

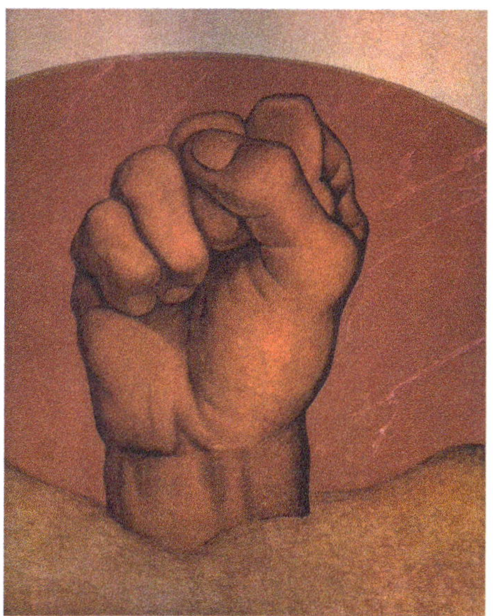

Diego Rivera, *Hand* (detail), National College of Agriculture, Chapingo, Mexico (1925–1927)

Ten years after I painted my first mural, I suffered my second crisis of faith. I doubted my abilities as an artist. But I also came to doubt the future of the mural movement with which I had identified. We seemed to be losing steam. We were less innovative than the graffiti writers who sometimes defaced our works. Theirs was a popular art, without all the representational apparatus of our mural painting. It seemed to capture the spirit of the streets better than ours did. Next to theirs, our work often looked tired and constrained.

The community mural movement developed as an outgrowth of the radical movements of the '60s. It flourished in the '70s and '80s as the momentum generated by those movements waned. By the '90s, the opportunities to paint murals with radical content were drying up. Even when walls were available, there wasn't the money to pay the artists to paint them.

The '60s had worked a profound cultural change in the United States, but it had not resulted in the transfer of power to "the people," nor had it narrowed the gap between the rich and the poor. Those elites who continued to hold the reins of power were not inclined to invite community muralists to decorate their corporate headquarters. The few commissions available from local governments were going to artists who could be counted on not to rock the boat.

Some of my fellow muralists emerged from the shadows cast by *Los Tres Grandes* to paint abstract or photorealistic murals; some incorporated graffiti. I felt I had nowhere to go with either my politics or my art, and quite to my surprise decided to go to law school. I no longer believed that I could avoid the dilemmas of modern art by collective work in a political context. The centrifugal forces pulling subject and object apart and undermining the synthesis inherent in aesthetic form could not be countered by the gravitational pull of political solidarity.

I was thrust back to the question I had left unanswered when I abandoned the Farewell to Art I'd started writing back in my railroad flat on the Lower East Side:

Is art dead, or dying, or just going though its usual changes?

Is Art Dead, Or Dying, Or Just Going through Its Usual Changes?

PAINTING IS EXPERIENCING a loss of the object. Object as purpose, as in "What is the object of this exercise?"; object as something out there in the world as in "I just tripped over that object on the sidewalk." The signs are everywhere.

I remember when I was still living in New York, walking up the great central stairway of the Metropolitan Museum to the galleries of European painting. I would stroll from room to room in a path that took me through the 15th, 16th, 17th, 18th, 19th, and 20th centuries until finally I would come to the capacious rooms in which hung the large abstract expressionist canvases of Klein, Pollock, DeKooning, Motherwell, and the quieter color field paintings of Rothko, Newman, Noland, and Still. Having reached this culminating point in my long trek to the present, I'd feel at first a great relief. In the presence of those great canvases, empty of all reference to objects, the paintings that I passed on the way to these rooms seemed small, dark, and cluttered. The royally furbished galleries in which they hung felt like storage lockers filled with overvalued junk. Good riddance, I thought. Let's have a garage sale. But then, after the relief, came a sense of "Well, now what?" Now that we've cleaned out the attic, what's left? Maybe we were a bit hasty. I didn't want to go back into the dark clutter of representation, but what was the way forward?

For centuries, artists created paintings that were worlds unto themselves, suffused with subjectivity. The work of art was an illusionary universe in which appearance and reality, object and subject were indivisible. The reconciliation of the self and the world that these works represented took place in the make-believe realm of the imagination. Nevertheless it held the promise of that reconciliation "in reality." I now sensed that reconciliation was no longer possible, even in the "unreal" realm of art. Art today veers between the pole of pure subjectivity unconstrained by the discipline of representation and the pole of an objectivity that treats subjectivity as a contaminant.

Abstract Expressionists such as DeKooning and Pollock slashed and splattered paint on canvases. The only guidance they accepted was that of the painting itself. They denied any obligation to reach out into the world for forms to follow. Outside of the feedback loop between the canvas and the artist nothing mattered and from outside nothing intruded. The phenomenal world was not re-presented. The painting became a playground, closed off to the outside world, but welcoming to the pure and spontaneous subjectivity of the artist. On its surface, like the footprints of children in the sandbox, were recorded the gestures that were the expression of that subjectivity.

Pop Art was Abstract Expressionism's antithesis. It took the omnipresent artifacts of our media-saturated environment—billboards, newspaper photographs, images of celebrities, panels from comic books—objects already inhabited with meaning, self-explanatory, and resisting interpenetration, and plopped them into galleries more or less as they were. Abstract Expressionism preferred its subjectivity unsullied by objects. Pop Art preferred its objects unsullied by subjectivity.* What both

* Andy Warhol preferred silkscreen to painting precisely because it was impersonal. He said "I wanted something . . . that gave more of an assembly-line effect." It was almost as if his personal touch would contaminate the work:

> [I]t was . . . his frequent practice to delegate the manual task of silkscreening an image onto canvas to his assistants. . . . By the 1970s Warhol no longer had any sustained involvement in the mass production of his paintings. "We had so much

Abstract Expressionism and Pop Art had in common is a distrust of the aesthetic dimension where the subject and object meet and interpenetrate. The art movements that have followed share this distrust.

Is it still possible for artists to create objects suffused with subjectivity in which the truth of our relationship to objects is neither distorted nor denied? Is art still capable of showing us how the self and the world can be reconciled? Is it still committed to that project? The art that's on display in today's museums of modern art and trend setting galleries gives no clear answers. It meanders blindly, leaving behind a trail of justifications and fancy language to cover its confusion. It may be that art must destroy all preconceptions we have about it before it can renew itself, but the destruction needs to contain the promise of renewal. That's not a promise it seems capable of making with any degree of conviction.

Transgression is the name of the game. Avant-garde art proceeds by a kind of brinksmanship. Each new wave transgresses on what has come before, always advancing—but toward what? The search is endless—for a new assumption to disprove, a new rule to violate. The art world flocks to view the latest episode of "art at risk," just as silent-movie goers flocked to the latest installment of *The Perils of Pauline*. There was Pauline, tied to the railroad tracks, the train bearing down on her, rescued at the last moment by our hero. Here's art, tied to convention, doomed for sure, but saved by the brave avant-garde artist who arrives in the nick of time, unties her, swings her up onto his saddle, and gallops off to freedom.

Art is dead, long live art. The problem is that after a number of episodes of art in peril the scenario becomes increasingly predictable. And boring. Shit or get off the pot. We get the message: There are no

> work [one of his assistants is quoted as saying], that even Augusto [the security man] was doing the painting. We were so busy that Andy and I did everything over the phone. We called it 'art by phone.'" One of the persons who is responsible for painting many of Warhol's later works . . . has said that Warhol's primary role in the creation of these paintings was simply to sign them when they were sold.

Richard Polsky "What Is an Andy Warhol?" *The New York Review of Books*, Volume 56, Number 16, October 22, 2009.

boundaries and no taboos. Rules are made to be broken. Art can be anything it wants to be. So why not admit: There is no reason to put a line, a color, a shape here rather than there. The choice is entirely arbitrary and increasingly meaningless.*

Already in the '60s, the art world, as it likes to think of itself, had begun to resemble the world of fashion. And it still does. Each new fad lasts for barely a season. The avant-garde becomes the old guard before the paint is dry on the canvas (assuming there are still artists retrograde enough to put paint on canvas). And just when it is no longer tenable to justify this cavalcade of fashion as the inevitable preordained progression of heroic avant-gardes and people are beginning to grumble and want their money back, it is decided that we are all "post-modern." The line of march loses its forward momentum, and the troops take off in all directions without leaders or followers, like Napoleon's snow-blinded army scattered by the blizzards of a Russian winter.

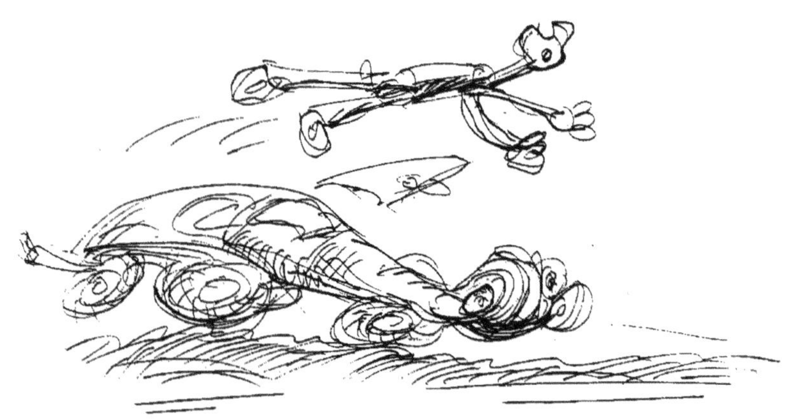

* "Today there is no shocking. The only thing shocking is no shocking." Marcel Duchamp quoted in John Berger, *The Moment of Cubism,* Pantheon Books: Random House, New York 1969, 51.

Art in the Age of Digital Reproduction

"The sight of immediate reality has become an orchid in the land of technology."

Walter Benjamin[39]

THE JOB OF the painter used to be clear and unproblematic: to present the world to us as it is and as it could be. For millennia there were no images without the painter. The world relied on painting to see itself. A painting was news. The painter's brush followed the contours of the world, carved forms from space and anointed them with color. There was power in the painter's art. It was a revelation. It was magic and science.

Painters are no longer needed to capture the moment and deliver it to us bound, shackled, and dressed in its Sunday best. They have been replaced by the most prolific hunter/gatherer of moments the world has ever known—the photographer.* She it is who bags the biggest game and brings home sacks full of trophies. At a thousandth of a second, she catches the speeding bullet in its flight.

We painters are obsolete. Bravely we soldier on, proclaiming ourselves relieved not to have the burden of representation and happy to be free to search for forms without any preconditions. We are like workers

* "Photographs are perhaps the most mysterious of all the objects that make up, and thicken, the environment we recognize as modern. Photographs really are experience captured, and the camera is the ideal arm of consciousness in its acquisitive mood. To photograph is to appropriate the thing photographed."
Susan Sontag, *On Photography*. New York: Farrar, Straus and Giroux, 1977, 3-4.

who have been replaced by mechanization, who insist they're delighted to be free of onerous obligations but soon find their lives lack structure or purpose. Identity crises follow. We put on a game face, all the while feeling that we're drowning. "We're free!" we cry. But free to do what? The truth of the matter is that painting is a charming anachronism, like blacksmithing and typesetting with movable type.

Technologically painting remains mired in the past. Painters are handcrafters. Our tools have changed little since the Renaissance. If the medium is the message, paint sends the wrong signals. A painting is dull compared to the glowing image on the silver screen. It is postage stamp small and never changes while all around us the world is in constant motion, lit up and electrified. Lasers split the sky and catalogue our purchases in the supermarket. Information radiates through the ether. Wondrous weightless technology rules the day. The materials from which an earlier era built a world—the globs of clay, the slabs of wood, the hunks of rock, and the multicolored goo on painters' palettes—are relegated to second-class citizenship.

As befits the mighty hunter of moments, the photographer has a weapon, which, compared to a paintbrush, is like a machine gun to a bow and arrow. The photographer *aims* the camera; she *shoots* and *captures* the moment. Her camera is constantly improving in speed and versatility. It can be swift and brutal, like the gun, but it can also seduce, manipulate, and improve upon reality. It can be as anonymous as a surveillance camera, or stamped with the personality of an Avedon or a Cartier-Bresson. But in either case, once photographers make the choice of what to shoot and click the shutter, the camera does the work. They're out of the picture. They can manipulate the image once it's shot, but if they're trying to convince us that the picture tells the truth, the manipulations will be concealed as if they were somehow shameful and illicit.

The painter is never out of the picture. The brush can not be aimed like the camera. As the blind move their hands over a face to discover its

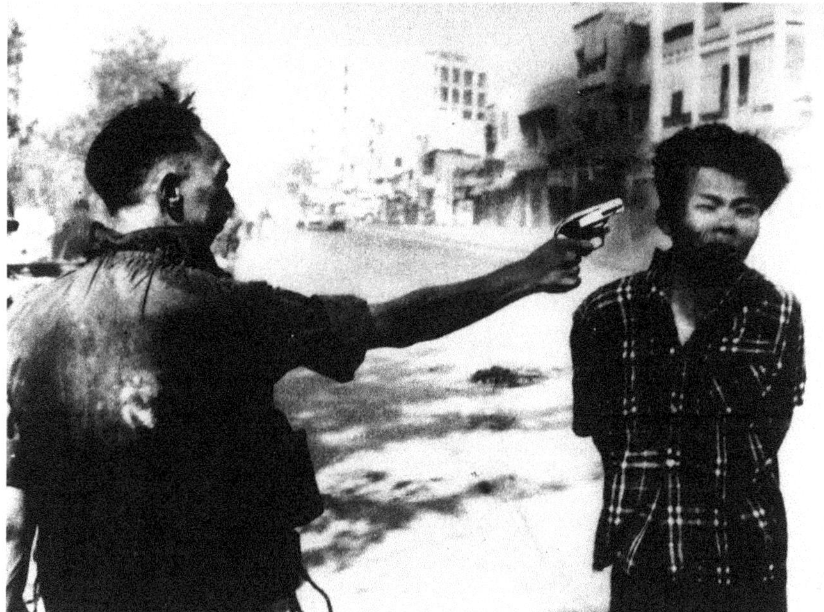

Eddie Adams, February 1, 1968. South Vietnam police chief Nguyen Ngoc Loan shoots a young man whom he suspects is a Viet Kong soldier.

features, so painters use a brush as an extension of their eyes. Their gaze moves over the contours of the world, and their brush follows.

Because the camera is neither conscious nor self-conscious and has no stake in the outcome of its operation, photography can claim to show us the way things *really* are. Painting can make no such claim. It gives us a world filtered through the medium of subjectivity. We say "a picture is worth a thousand words," but a painting has nowhere near the value of a photograph as evidence.* Eddie Adams' searing photograph of the execution of a suspected Viet Cong soldier captures the exact moment

* "Between two fantasy alternatives, that Holbein the Younger had lived long enough to have painted Shakespeare or that a prototype of the camera had been invented early enough to have photographed him, most Bardolators would choose the photograph. This is not just because it would presumably show what Shakespeare really looked like, for even if the hypothetical photograph were faded, barely legible, a brownish shadow, we would probably still prefer it to another glorious Holbein. Having a photograph of Shakespeare would be like having a nail from the True Cross."

Susan Sontag, *On Photography*. New York: Farrar, Straus and Giroux, 1978, 154.

that the bullet enters his skull. Adams was there. He saw it with his own eyes. His camera is an unimpeachable witness.*

On the other hand there is no evidence that Goya was a witness to the executions that he depicts in *The Third of May, 1808: The Execution of the Defenders of Madrid.*

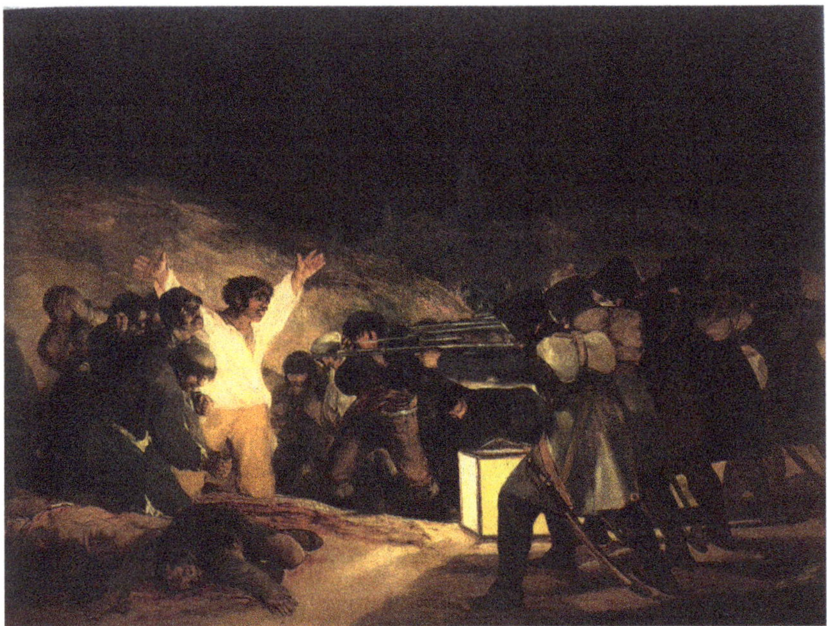

Francisco Goya, *The Third of May 1808* (1814)

* Adams won the 1969 Pulitzer Prize for this photograph. He later questioned whether the photograph told the whole truth. He wrote in *Time Magazine:*

> The general killed the Viet Cong; I killed the general with my camera. Still photographs are the most powerful weapon in the world. People believe them; but photographs do lie, even without manipulation. They are only half-truths. . . . What the photograph didn't say was, "What would you do if you were the general at that time and place on that hot day, and you caught the so-called bad guy after he blew away one, two, or three American people?"

Eddie Adams, "Eulogy: General Nguyen Ngoc Loan," *Time Magazine*, July 27, 1998.

It's odd to expect a photograph to answer a "what if" question. The fact that it can't doesn't turn it into a lie. Were there to be a trial of the general for war crimes, his defense attorney might ask the jury, "What would you have done if you were in his place?" He wouldn't ask the photograph. It's just evidence, silent witness, available to defense and prosecution alike.

He painted the picture six years after the event took place. The truth of his painting is not the truth of a reliable eyewitness. It's a truth about light in the midst of darkness, sacrifice, resistance, and the vulnerability of flesh. Monet's water lilies aren't treasured as evidence. We don't much care what the lily pond at Giverny looked like at the end of the 19th century unless we are specialists in the history of gardening; we turn to Monet to experience shimmering light, fragile as a butterfly wing, reinvented as a timeless radiance.

Photography has achieved its supremacy over painting without attempting to compete with it on its own terms. Or rather, sometimes it competes and sometimes it doesn't. On the question of whether it should be considered an art or not, photography straddles the fence. At times it dons the mantle of high art. It's happy when museums embrace it as an "art form" and set aside galleries to display what are considered great photographs, beautifully framed and matted. At other times, it mounts a populist revolt against aesthetics. Its aesthetic value lies precisely in the fact that it abjures aesthetics. It doesn't bathe the facts of life in the slobber of subjectivity.* Photography is a democratic medium. Anyone with a digital camera can unleash a flood of pictures. One commentator estimated that

> * "[T]he very question of whether photography is or is not an art is essentially a misleading one. Although photography generates works that can be called art—it requires subjectivity, it can lie, it gives aesthetic pleasure—photography is not, to begin with, an art form at all. Like language, it is a medium in which works of art (among other things) are made. Out of language, one can make scientific discourse, bureaucratic memoranda, love letters, grocery lists, and Balzac's Paris. Out of photography, one can make passport pictures, weather photographs, pornographic pictures, x-rays, wedding pictures, and Atget's Paris. Photography is not an art like, say, painting and poetry. Although the activities of some photographers conform to the traditional notion of a fine art, the activity of exceptionally talented individuals producing discrete objects that have value in themselves, from the beginning photography has also lent itself to that notion of art which says that art is obsolete. The power of photography—and its centrality in the present aesthetic concerns—is that it confirms both ideas of art. But the way in which photography renders art obsolete is, in the long run, stronger."
>
> Susan Sontag *On Photography*, 148

Sontag is clearly wrong when she says that photography is not an art form, but "a language." One can speak loosely of line, color, and form as the "language," of visual images, but it's a language shared by photography, painting, and all visual arts.

375 billion digital photographs would be taken in 2011. The total number of photographs ever taken? He thinks 3.5 trillion. [40]

That's too many. The downside of all that capturing is that the world no longer calls out to be represented. We are drowning in representations. In van Gogh's time, the relation of art to the world could be symbolized by a few feet of stretched canvas on an easel sitting in a vast landscape. He painted in a wheat field outside of Arles, and the only image for miles around was the one on his easel. Today, fields of wheat have been replaced by fields of images, more numerous than grains of wheat. Imagescape has replaced landscape. We drown in a glossy, full-color sea of representations, Photoshopped, stomach churning, and set to music.

An encounter with the natural world—with sky and earth, water and rock, sunlight and shadow—is an encounter with depth and resonances. Our presence suffuses nature with an indeterminate meaningfulness, as palpable as the murmur of brooks and the buzz of honeybees. The glory of oil paint is its ability to convey the depth and resonances of the natural world. In a biblical scene by Rembrandt, a portrait by Velazquez, a still life by Zurbaran, or a candle-lit interior by de la Tour, the eye snuggles into luminous glazes of oil paint like a cat into a soft pillow.

The processed world of digitized, pixilated, multiply-copied images that surrounds us is a world of surfaces, a world without depth or inwardness. It comes with ready made meanings to which we do not contribute. We could die of starvation beneath the billboard advertising breakfast cereals. We could have a heart attack watching television and the smile of the actress in the toothpaste commercial would not waiver.

The stars in the night sky are also oblivious to our suffering, but at least they don't pretend to care. To paint this world of images with oils in the manner of the great masters would be absurd. To paint this world at all may be absurd.

The overpopulating representations feed on each other. Photography, the great hunter/gatherer has been so successful, that there is barely any fresh game left in the forest. Like vultures on carrion, images feed on images. Their point of origin is no longer a reality that precedes and is independent of representation. We used to think of trees as the precursors of all pictures of trees. Now, if the last tree were clear-cut we would continue to enjoy a forest of tree images, under whose sheltering boughs long-extinct animals would mingle with murderers and movie stars. Endangered species prolong their tenuous existence on Sierra Club calendars. Politicians exist as images on TV and in the newspaper. If by chance we catch a glimpse of one "in real life," we are shocked to encounter, in the space of our lived experience, the template from which all the familiar images are struck. Police officers, smoking cigarettes and lounging outside the station house, have learned how police are supposed to act from actors in the movies who, in turn, have learned from the police, who learned from the movies and so on.* Representation precedes reality. The portrait determines the portrayed. In our moments of greatest crisis we think, "It's just like in the movies."

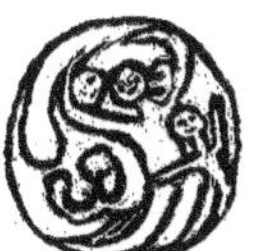

Our realty is shaped by an all encompassing system of economic, political and cultural institutions—capitalist, patriarchal, racist, however you wish to characterize it. It is a system in which the rich wage unequal war against the poor, steal the fruits of their labor, and despoil the earth in the process. The system is not simply an external set of relations between people and things. It infects subjectivity. It must at all costs conceal the truth that a better world is possible. It manufactures consent, through

* And not just police. "*The Godfather*—both Francis Ford Coppola's movie and Mario Puzo's book—was a sacred text for a whole generation of Bulgarian gangsters and Stoev [who was killed after writing an exposé of the gangster life] was happy to be given a chance to become a fiction character. It was an offer, one might say, that he couldn't refuse." (Dimitre Kenarov, "Chronicle of a Death Foretold," *The Nation,* May 18, 2009, 25.)

force and fear, but largely through the images with which it infects the mind. The flood of images produced by digital photography may occasionally reveal a truth the powers that be would prefer to hide. But it also serves to hide the truth and to distract us. Instead of the power to change the world, we are given the chance to snap its picture. At most demonstrations, especially the ones that involve some risk, participants will be outnumbered by people taking their photograph. In order for the truth to emerge, we sometimes must tear through the veil of images that infect our mind to the invisible that lies beneath. The world must be shaken and shocked into revelation.

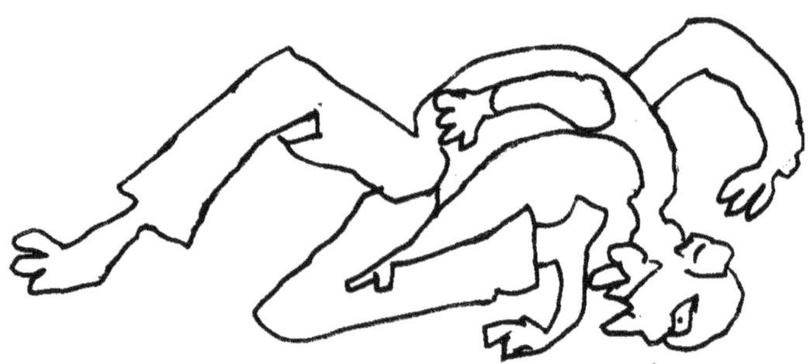

Art in the Age of Melting Glaciers

IS IT MERELY a coincidence that just as we are in the process of drowning reality in its representations, ecological catastrophe looms and we drown nature in the waste products of our consumption?

Humanity is facing a crisis. That crisis is not far off in the distant future. It shadows the present. The biological basis of life is threatened. We have abused the earth and can no longer take for granted that she'll always be there to meet our needs like a battered woman who continues to prepare breakfast for her husband.

A deadly atavistic irrationality, spawn of reason and its destroyer, perhaps the fruit of some latent tropism toward death deep in the heart of our species, now asserts itself against countervailing forces that seek to preserve life. I fear that none of our efforts will be sufficient to steer the ark of human civilization toward safe harbor. That ark, which we have constructed over millennia, fought over, and wrestled to control, is too large to turn on a dime. I fear that those at the helm are too short-sighted to see the peril that lies ahead. I fear that those who see the danger will not succeed in seizing control of the tiller while there's still time to wrench the vessel from its collision course with nature.

What lies ahead? Has the tipping point been reached? Is it too late to avoid the extinction of our species? Will all we have built collapse in a churning, frantic, clawing, bitter crush? The question is too large to face. It sucks all the oxygen from the room in which hope struggles to survive.

All previous catastrophes have been imaginable. They have had comprehensible causes and effects. But this global catastrophe has too many causes. Previous catastrophes have been local—a heat wave, a hurricane, a drought, a deluge. Their full extent and power is immediately known by those whose lives are affected. But this catastrophe is different. We cannot verify it by our experience. We can surmise that a heat wave or a hurricane or a drought or a deluge is a symptom of global warming, but we can only know that the temperature of the entire earth is rising as a result of human activity by assembling data and relying on its interpretation by experts. There is therefore abundant opportunity for doubt. Perhaps the climate modelers are wrong, and we are experiencing only a temporary rise in the temperature caused by some wobble of the earth, and not by our misdeeds. Perhaps the graph of rising global temperature more closely resembles the path of a drunken sailor meandering down the sidewalk than a hockey stick. No certainties here. Only perhapses. We experience weather, but not the incremental changes in climate. We proceed with our lives as if . . . as if nothing had changed. We fall back on old habits.

But over all hangs a pall. Our children are unsure they have a future. In the past, prophets of doom have been criers of wolf. Guys with beards carrying signs "The End Is Nigh" feature prominently in *New Yorker* cartoons. But never has humanity had at its disposal technologies of such immense power. The smoke from Blake's "dark Satanic Mills" could blacken the sky over London and rain soot upon its tenements, but it dissipated in the wild blue yonder. Blake could not have foreseen that all the earth would come to resemble a sooty mill town, its air thick with the byproducts of combustion, its waters polluted by the toxic spew of manufacturing.

He cried:

> Bring me my bow of burning gold:
> Bring me my arrows of desire:

> Bring me my spear: O clouds unfold!
> Bring me my chariot of fire.
> I will not cease from mental fight,
> Nor shall my sword sleep in my hand
> Till we have built Jerusalem
> In England's green and pleasant land.
>
> —William Blake, *Jerusalem* from the preface to *Milton, a Poem* (1808)

The "green and pleasant land" has never been more in need of champions with swords unsheathed.

> We have two paths: either Pachamama or death.
> We have two paths: either capitalism dies or Mother Earth dies.
> Either capitalism lives or Mother Earth lives.
> Of course, brothers and sisters, we are here for life,
> for humanity and for the rights of Mother Earth.
> Long live the rights of Mother Earth! Death to capitalism![41]

Thus spoke Evo Morales, the Aymara Indian President of Bolivia, at the opening of the World Peoples' Summit on Climate Change and Rights of Mother Earth, in Tiquipaya outside of Cochabamba, Bolivia on April 20, 2010.

If Evo is right, and there are only two paths: the one in which capitalism lives till nature dies; the other in which capitalism is overthrown in time for nature to survive, then indeed we are in dire straits. Fredric Jameson once wrote, "It seems easier for us today to imagine the thoroughgoing deterioration of the earth and of nature than the breakdown of late capitalism; and perhaps that is due to some weakness in our imaginations."[42]

Perhaps. But if, as many climate scientists warn, we cannot wait twenty, thirty, or forty years for the breakdown of capitalism, and, if further, we consider that it must happen in such a way that what is unleashed is not a atavistic earth-swallowing barbarism, but loving kindness toward nature and all her children, then it's hard to blame our imagination for its weakness. In 1967, when I gave up art, I believed that its promise could be fulfilled on earth and that the imagination need no longer be confined to a little area, fenced off from reality by the borders of the canvas. Now it is not the possibility of liberation, but the ultimate betrayal of that possibility, which throws into question art's promise that a better world is possible.

In the face of a looming threat to the biological basis of our life on earth, the making of art sometimes feels like the grooming activity of a mouse trapped in a maze. Nothing we can do as artists is commensurate with the enormity of that onrushing disaster. Art shows us the universal in the individual—all suffering in a crucifixion by Grünewald, all the vitality of youth in Michelangelo's *David*. But the greatest horrors cannot be represented. There is no way to turn them into art without diminishing them. Language itself fails in the face of the most unspeakable catastrophes. Torture and genocide become "human rights violations"; the destruction of the biological bases of life becomes "anthropogenic climate change"—the pale abstractions are the ghosts of the reality. The forms which art has at its disposal are incapable of grasping the unimaginable. Art cannot help itself. It humanizes what it touches. And the extinction of the species cannot be humanized. The question of whether it is possible to make art after Auschwitz needs to be asked again in the context of forces that threaten to turn the Earth into a death camp.

Art has always been the hope of the hopeless, the refuge of those without shelter, the joy of the bitterly sorrowful. Without hope, there can be no art; and without art, there can be no hope. When all hope is lost, we seek solace in a song. The mother whose child is dying in her arms will, in its last moments, croon a lullaby to sooth it toward sleep. And if we, as humanity, are killing our mother, we might as well croon a lullaby to ourselves, and rock ourselves in each other's arms, as we descend into the everlasting sleep of the human race.

But what sort of a lullaby? Will it have melody or will it resemble an inarticulate, unmusical cry?

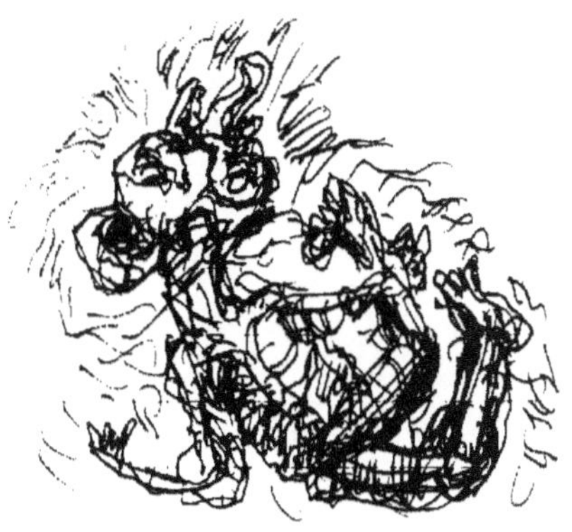

Global warming is a sign that we have put itself on a course that is irreconcilable with nature, the nature of rivers and oceans, sky and earth, plants and animals. But also *our* nature. Nature is putty in our hands. We have that much power. We have used it to create not a pleasant habitation, but an execution chamber. Why? The labor that should have made us more human has dehumanized us; the work that should have enriched us has impoverished us all.

If humanity is at war with nature, can artists continue to produce forms that speak of the reconciliation between the self and the world? A work of art can either confront or deny the truth of our relationship to the world. If it denies the truth, and pretends an easy reconciliation between the self and the world, then it will be a lie.

If we can no longer look out at the world and see a reflection of ourselves, then we can no longer paint the gas station across the street, our own face in the mirror, or a bowl of fruit as if the world was unchanged and history was something that happened somewhere else. The forms we find—or that find us—express the essential nature of our being in the world, with all its rifts and fissures.*

These days art speaks for humanity when it says: I am not in harmony with the world. I will not be reconciled with the irreconcilable. I untie the knot. I demand a divorce.

All of us have affections, friendships, and familiar objects that give us pleasure. If we are lucky we take vacations and find enjoyment in some small piece of relatively unspoiled nature. But our relation to this world of our familiars is not emblematic of our relation to our times, to the historical matrix in which we are embedded, to the powers that be and the world they have made in their detestable image.

Perhaps I want to paint a still life. Before me, on a table is a bowl of fruit. I like fruit. I like the way it looks and tastes. It probably doesn't look all that different to me than it did to a Dutch still life painter of the 17th century. But how am I going to paint it? If I paint it at all—which is unlikely—I might paint it as if I had no obligation to it, as if the bowl of fruit and I were infinitely separate, as separate as I am from my government and the atrocities it perpetrates in my name. I might begin by drawing lines that follow the curve of an apple and mimic the ellipse of a bowl, but soon I'd begin to wonder what's the point. Let the line wander as it will. What would be lost? Why not smash the bowl and crumple up

* "The work is never limited to the painted, sculpted, or narrated object. Just as one perceives things only against the background of the world, so the objects represented by art appear against the background of the universe. . . . If the painter presents us with a field or a vase of flowers, his paintings are windows which are open on the whole world. We follow the red path which is buried among the wheat much farther than van Gogh has painted it, among other wheat fields, under other clouds, to the river which empties into the sea, and we extend to infinity, to the other end of the world, the deep finality which supports the existence of the field and the earth. So that, through the various objects which it produces or reproduces, the creative act aims at a total renewal of the world. Each painting, each book, is a recovery of the totality of being. Each of them presents this totality to the freedom of the spectator. For this is quite the final goal of art: to recover this world by giving it to be seen as it is, but as if it had its source in human freedom." Jean-Paul Sartre, *What Is Literature?* trans. Bernard Frechtman. New York: Philosophical Library, 1949, 57.

the drawing? The smashed pieces of pottery and crumpled pieces of paper would more truly reflect my relation to the world than a painting in which I respectfully mimic its forms and colors. I could put the crumpled pieces of paper and smashed fragments of pottery in a frame and call it still life. Who's to stop me? The world is not my mirror, or my friend.

Art today disavows unity. It embraces dissonance; it's fragmentary and distrustful of all boundaries. It finds the smarmy harmonies of traditional art banal and irrelevant. All those noble reconciliations within the frame, those peace treaties between the self and the world, what have they done but permit the world to continue on its despicable course? They decorate its atrocities. They provide solace for its torturers and their eager enablers. They make the unbearable bearable.

The meaning of representation is that the self and world can be reconciled while the world remains as it is; the wound can be healed while the plague continues. But it can't. So why bother? There is no safe haven. We make no separate peace. Behold art the destroyer.

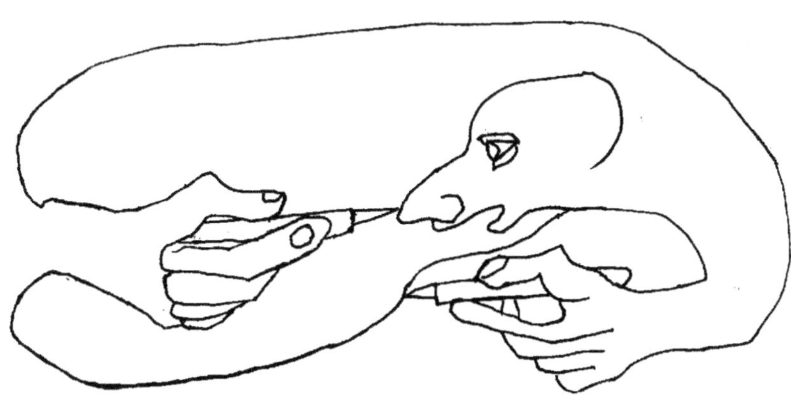

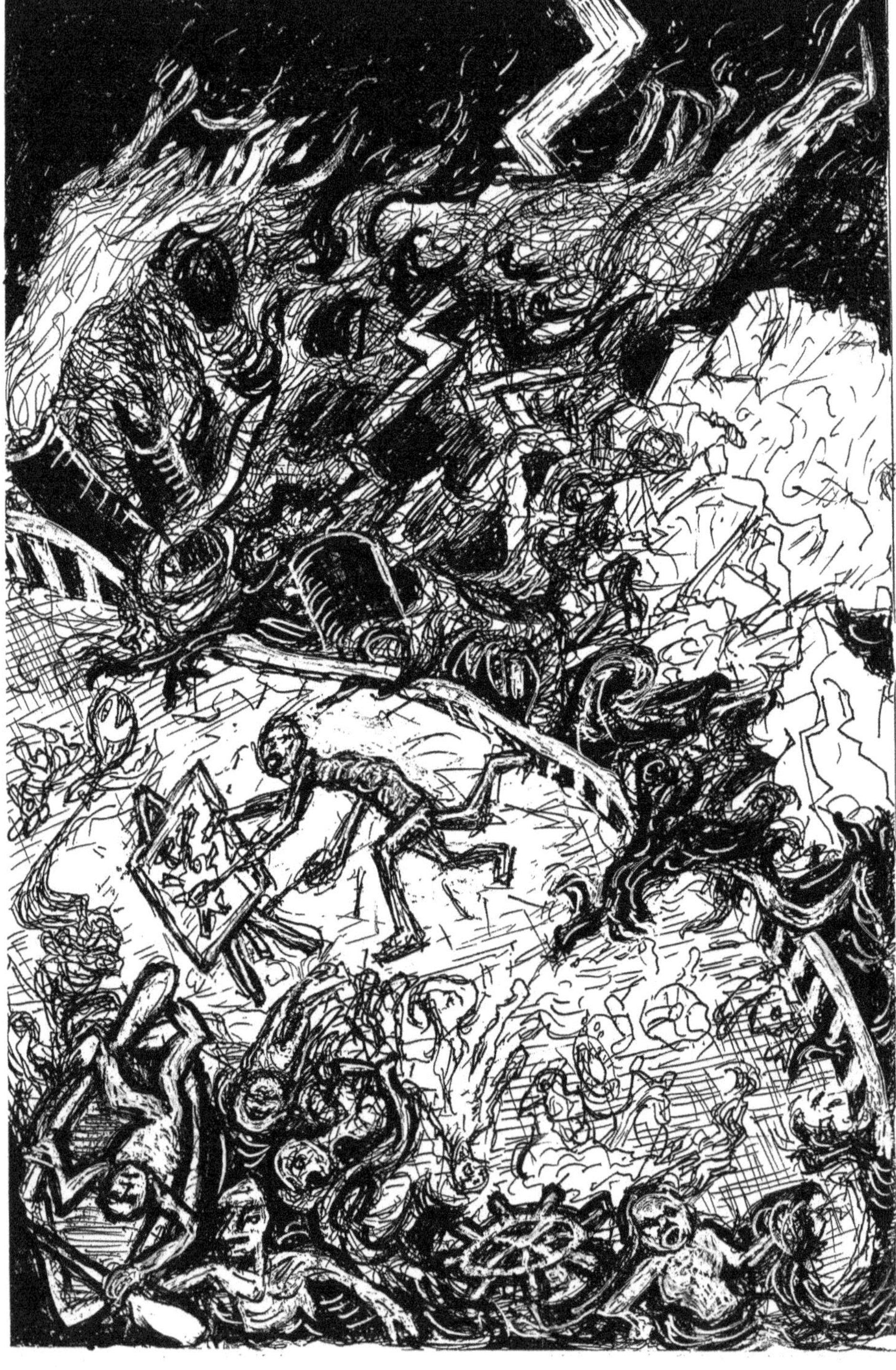

Art in the Age of Genetic Modification

WE DO NOT know when human beings began forming the stuff of the world into images and articles of adornment. Pierced shell "beads" found in a Moroccan cave appear to be 82,000 years old.[43] The cave lions, cave hyenas, panthers, cave bears, owls, horses, cattle, and rhinoceroses painted on the walls of the cave of Chauvet in southern France are currently thought to be between 35,000 and 30,000 years old. The sureness with which each species is characterized suggests the paintings are the work of artists who inherited a tradition that stretched back multiple millennia.

Perhaps the impulse to make such images is as old as our species. Whenever it may have been that the first human drew a design in the sand with her finger, then stopped and looked at what she had done and took pleasure in it, we humans have persisted without interruption and under the most varied conditions in the creation of objects whose forms embody our visions and imaginings and which satisfy something deep within us by their very presence. These objects, to which we now give the name of art, constitute a veritable rainforest under whose canopy we shelter from a life that would otherwise be too harsh and unfulfilling.

But just as the rainforest of the Amazon, which has endured in its vastness for millennia, is now burnt and chastened, and trembles before threats unique in its history, just as it breathes for the first time the putrid air of its own extinction, so the fecund rainforest of artistic forms appears to be in trouble.

When we conduct a careful examination of art's ecosystem we notice troubling changes. An invasive mutant species is proliferating, endangering the fauna and flora of the forest by crowding the ecological niches in which they once flourished. The mutant is consuming the reality which is art's food supply, leaving it nothing to feed on but itself. It has two main subspecies, advertising and entertainment, but in various forms it can be found wherever processed information is communicated. Webster's definition of media—"all the means of communication, as newspapers, radio, and TV, to provide the public with news, entertainment, etc., usually along with advertising."—is a good description of the mutation. All its forms are related, just as all breeds of dogs—the cuddly and the fierce, the floppy-eared and the pug-nosed, the Great Danes and the Chihuahuas—are all *canis lupus,* share a common genetic profile, and are capable of interbreeding.

This media mutation is a marvel of genetic engineering, created by splicing the DNA of art to that of a proliferative, invasive species. It is useful to corporations in a way that art has never been. But can it really be distinguished from art? Is it really a separate species? Undeniably, it's art-like, sometimes very art-like; sometimes it resembles bad art; sometimes it seems like the very antithesis of art; and sometimes, to add to the confusion, evolution works backwards and a creation of the media that was thought to carry the mutant's DNA is recognized as a new shoot springing from the old-growth forest of art, attesting to its continuing vitality.

The too-muchness of this art-like mutation, its penetration into all the nooks and crannies of our life, its lack of boundaries, is what make it so deadly. It has invaded every corner of the globe and the intimate privacy of our thoughts. It reaches directly into our soul, interpreting the world, pleasuring our senses, and exciting our imagination. It has replaced the knobby knees of reality with eroticized simulacra.

What's left of art has become the mutant's farm system, nursery, and gene pool. Art that rages against what-is in the name of what-might-be is instantly absorbed and fed directly into its veins. The mutant loves what resists it. With infinite subtlety it takes the forms generated by an art that reflects our alienation and absorbs their DNA. It feeds on outsiders. It depends on them for its renewal. It loves artistic rebels, their heads woozy with antiquated dreams of heroic avant-gardes. Twist and shout as they may, those would-be rebels cannot escape its strangling embrace. It clamps onto them and sucks their juices. The outrages of surrealists sell underwear.

With the development of capitalism, art became a commodity, bought and sold like any other; but paradoxically, it's been a commodity, which is valued because it provides a relief from the buying and selling of commodities. It does not have a use, like butter and toaster ovens. It can't do what they do, and they can't do what it does. We would not confuse a pound of butter with a work of art.

Or would we? What if the butter comes in a carton decorated with pictures of rolling hills and smiling farmers? What if the commercial for butter is a three-minute opera with dancing cows, flowering meadows, and angelic choruses swelling as the camera pans to a close-up of a melting yellow pad atop the brown bosom of a stack of pancakes?

Ad agencies have *art* departments whose sole purpose is to transfer art's DNA to commodities. Art arrays the nakedness of the world in the vestments of desire. The world is re-presented as if it were no longer other and apart. It is remade in our image. But now the utopian promise of art has become the siren song of the supermarket shelves. Cleaning products promise not just cleanliness, but a loving home where the silver sparkles. Communications technology promises not just communication, but community. Alcoholic beverages promise glamor and a hot date. A car is a woman inviting men to enter her. A truck is a good buddy, clapping us on our back with a brawny protective arm. This vast world of commodities is a packaged dream by which we are seduced and abandoned. We are seldom unaware of its fraudulence, but we are seduced anyway. The truth of the production of commodities is a cold calculation of profit and loss. The mutant commodity, decked out as a work of art, purports to do what art has always done—greet us as if we were its long-lost friend. But the promises of commodities, art-like as they may be, are never kept. Nor were they meant to be. They are dreamed up by cynical people who don't believe them. We are sold a bill of goods.

Meanwhile the misery of our lives continues unabated, alleviated only fleetingly by our activities as docile consumers and the small pleasures of our private lives. None of the endless commodities we consume actually reduce our misery. They smile on us as we scream in agony and tremble in loneliness. We reach out for consolation and a digital voice asks us to "please hold for the next available operator." Instead of intimacy we get pornography. The world of commodities puts on the mask of an old pal, but it's not our friend.

The mutant, which has transferred art's potent DNA to commodities, is everywhere. It leaks into our lives. We sit in front of the computer screen for hours, surfing the web, playing games, and watching videos. We watch television more than is good for us. With our finger on the remote, we turn the alternating current of programs and commercials into an endless flow in which nothing is complete and there are no boundaries. Rarely do we watch a program from beginning to end. When we're out of the house we play with our very smart phones, giving our thumbs a workout. When driving, our eyes wander to the billboards. And even if we don't have a TV and only use our computer at work or to check our e-mail, there is no escape. Freed from the frame that always contained a work of art, the mutant commodity slimes our entire existence.

Images created in conscious opposition to the universe of debased images with which we are surrounded nevertheless remain images, and therefore are as much a part of the problem as the solution. Throughout the centuries, there have been artists who have painted against the dominant forms of representation, and by so doing have subverted expectations and renewed the imagination. But it is questionable whether art is still capable of renewing our imagination sufficiently to allow it to break free from an all-encompassing and terrifying reality.

Art, the domain of freedom, turns into its opposite. Its truth is in bondage to a lie. If beauty is the promise of happiness, the mutant purports to be, not just the promise, but its fulfillment. Entertainment is art without a boundary, distance, or estrangement. Advertising promises immediate gratification. Art promises a freedom not yet possible in reality. The mutant uses that promise to lure us into slavery.

Art struggles against absorption by the mutant, but in the process risks tearing itself apart. It flirts with suicide. Its first job is the destruction of an enveloping matrix of illusion. But art that is only about destruction turns into anti-art. In the end, there must be a place of rest and jubilation.

Those of us who still believe in the power of art are like rescue workers, who, refusing to give up hope, search through the wreckage left by an earthquake for signs of life. Perhaps our hope is misplaced. Perhaps it is no longer possible for art to stand against the world in any significant way. The scandals of modern art fade before they blossom. The outrages of Impressionism provide decorative placemats for fast-food restaurants. Van Gogh's wheat fields go well in the kitchens of suburban tract houses. His yellows complement the trim. His work is best seen in glossy reproductions. The actual canvases are tired, small, and somewhat sad.*

* "Painting as we know it? I think it has no future in our civilization. Neither does sculpture. What we might call "bad painting"—that has a future . . . There will always be people who would like to have a picturesque landscape, or a nude, or a bouquet of flowers hanging on the wall . . . but what we call great painting is finished." (Alberto Giacometti, cited in James Lord, *Giacometti: A Biography*. New York: Noonday Press, 1985, 447.)
Will the same someday be said of film?

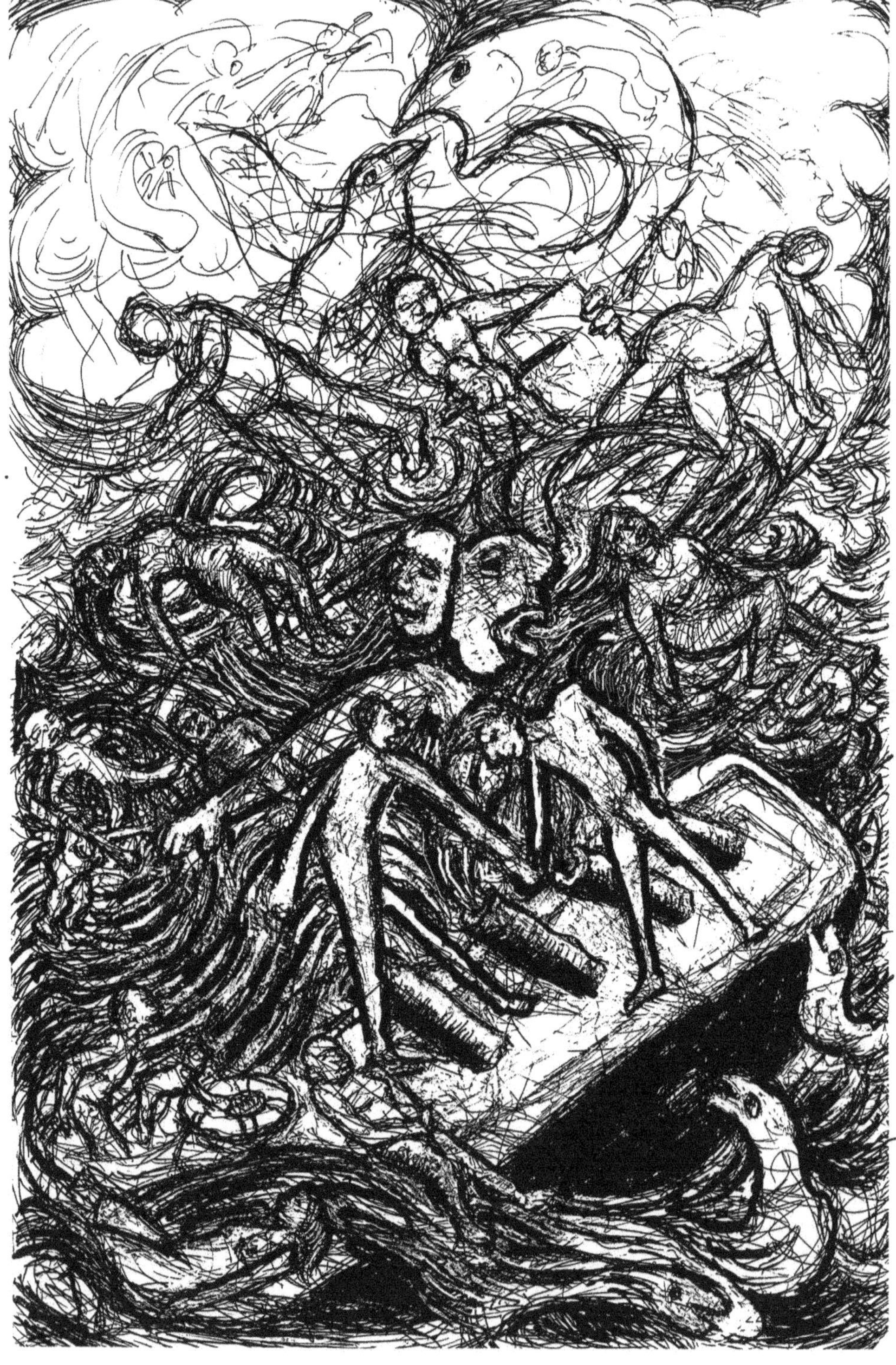

In The End, I Keep Drawing

The patron saint of painters, St. Luke himself, doctor, painter and Evangelist, whose symbol alas is nothing better than an ox, is there to encourage us. Yet in our real, true life we painters are quite humble, vegetating under the crushing yoke of a profession which is scarcely practicable on this thankless planet, on whose surface "the love of art means loss of true love."

But as there is no proof to the contrary—and presupposing, of course, in the innumerable other planets and suns, the existence of lines, forms, and colors—we are free to maintain a cheerfulness with regard to the possibility of painting under better and changed conditions of existence, an existence changed by a phenomenon no more tricky or astonishing than the transformation of a caterpillar into a butterfly, or of a white grub into a cockchafer.

The field of action of our metamorphosed butterfly-painter would be one of the many stars which, after death, are probably no more inaccessible to us than the little black dots on maps which, in our terrestrial existence, stand for towns and villages.

Vincent van Gogh, Letter to Emile Bernard, last week of June 1888[44]

There is an art of the future, and it is going to be so lovely and so young that even if we give up our youth for it we must gain in serenity by it.

Vincent van Gogh, Letter to Theo van Gogh[45]

I'M SITTING IN my office. It's evening. I'm drawing and I'm thinking about art. The thoughts are liquid and indeterminate. I concentrate on my drawing. I do not feel the *Zeitgeist* tugging at my arm, directing my marker pen in one direction or another. Outside on the sidewalk the trash is stacked for tomorrow's pickup. Across the street, the choir is leaving the church after its regular Wednesday night practice. Car doors slam. Radios play.

I have hope that we may be entering another period of revolution, but as yet the streets outside my window do not tremble with the thunder of feet rushing to the barricades. Mighty currents of discontent, renewed daily by the suppression of our legitimate hopes, flow just beneath the surface of daily life. They will not remain submerged forever.

Alone in my office I keep drawing. My drawings represent a sort of compromise. They could slash and splatter abstractly across the page. They could adhere minutely to appearances, mimicking the shapes of things in the world. They could lose themselves in the dance of unfettered emotion; they could embrace an anonymous geometry. They do what they do. I'm not sure why. The drawings themselves must provide the answer. So it has always been and so, we hope, it will always be. Whether art will survive, and, if so, in what form and with what power, are questions which only art itself can answer.

I am of two minds on the subject. On the one hand I believe that the fate of art and the fate of social movements for human liberation are linked. Not that art can be, or should be, in some simplistic sense, a tool of the revolution, but that without vital social movements capable of transforming the world, art can only hurl its body against a world in which art becomes increasingly impossible. Ultimately the logic of art that stands alone against the atrocity of global capitalism seems to lead to art's annihilation—to silence. And only in the space opened up by subversion and revolutionary change can art escape that logic.

That's on the one hand. On the other, I can no more imagine human beings ceasing to sing, dance, and adorn themselves and their world than I can imagine them ceasing to eat and breathe. The end of art? Impossible. What could I have been thinking?

Is art in danger? Life is in danger. The commodity culture of global capitalism is omnivorous. The beast swallows us all. It makes a meal of us. We hope it chokes. We make songs as we roil about in its guts. We doodle as it consumes us for breakfast. We dance as we are excreted from its bowels. Hurray and hurrah. So may it always be.

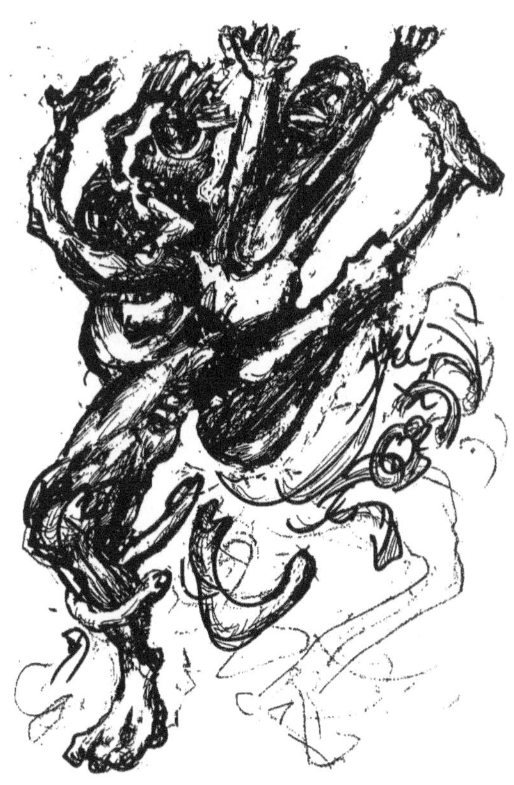

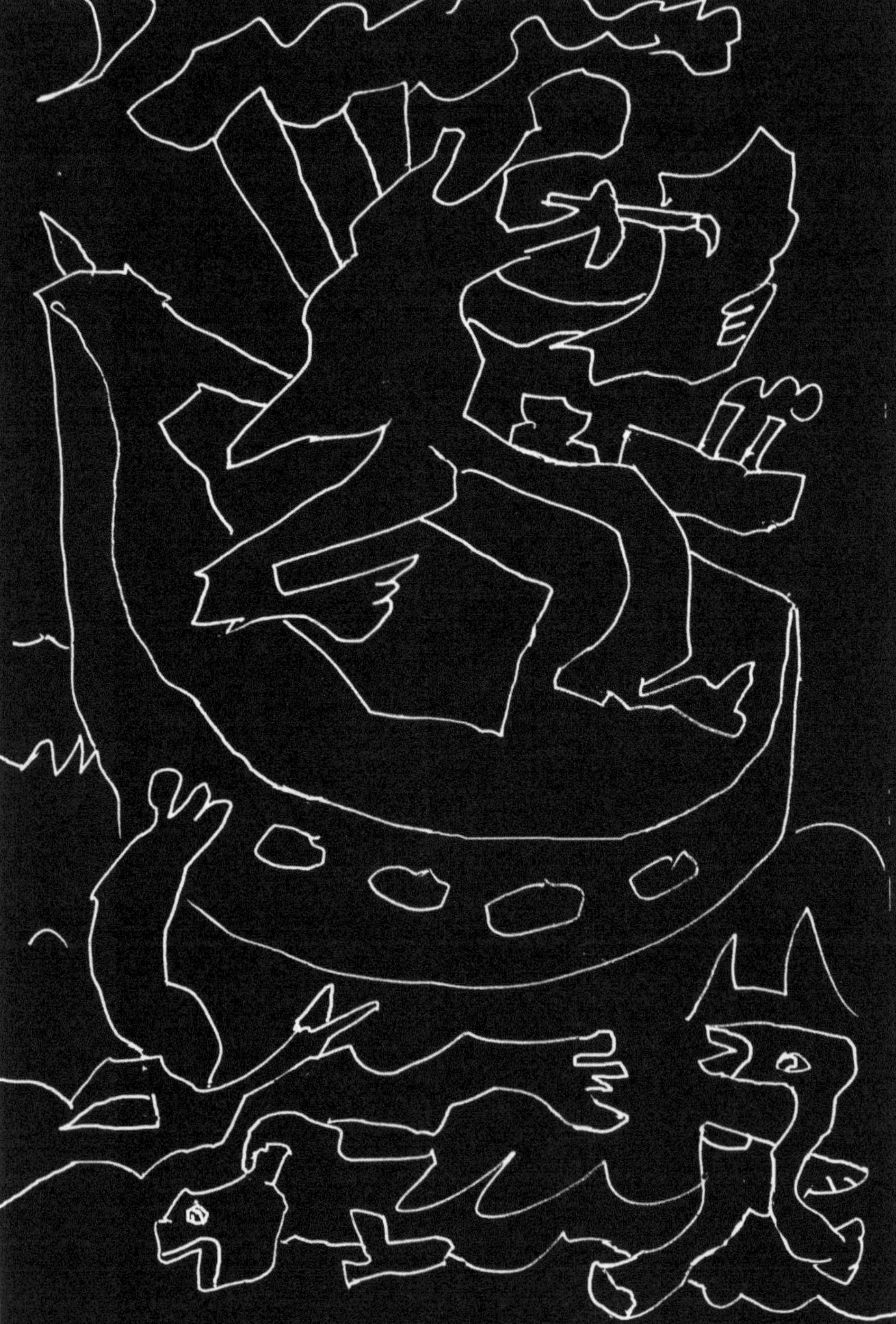

Appendix
Herbert Marcuse and the Aesthetic Dimension

HERBERT MARCUSE WAS not an artist, but he had a deep respect for art. He wrote one poem that I know of when my mother Inge died. He liked music, but did not feel particularly confident that he understood it, deferring to his colleague at the Frankfurt Institute, Theodor Adorno, in that department. Chamber music by Schubert, Beethoven, and Mozart took up much of the space in our record cabinet. A small shelf toward the bottom held recordings of Paul Robeson and Burl Ives, Lotte Lenya singing Kurt Weil, and *Songs of the Lincoln Brigade.* I remember in the living room and dining room beautiful reproductions of a Canaletto view of the *Piazza San Marco* and Bruegel's *Fall of Icarus.* We also had a couple of original etchings by Chagall, and, best of all to my mind, a Käthe Kollwitz woodcut, *Memorial to Karl Liebknecht,* which was stolen from Marcuse and my mother's house in La Jolla after he died. His great love was literature. He wrote his dissertation on the German *Künstlerroman,* the art novel. Of writers that were his contemporaries he loved Brecht and Beckett.

Marcuse was fond of the saying of Stendhal, "*La beauté n'est que la promesse du bonheur*" (beauty is the promise of happiness). He believed that, given the present conditions of human existence, there had to be a boundary between art and life if art was to preserve that promise. Again and again in his writings, he defended art's autonomy, even against those whose aim was to fulfill beauty's promise of happiness *in reality.*

The Aesthetic Dimension: Toward a Critque of Marxist Aesthetics, Herbert Marcuse's last book, is a slim volume of no more than 88 pages. In it he mounts his final defense of art as an autonomous realm that must stand aside from life if it is to preserve, against the world as it is, the promise of a better world awaiting. The aesthetic dimension for Marcuse is a realm of freedom. It is free because within it the only laws are the laws that determine the form of a work of art, and those laws are unknown and unknowable except in so far as we sense them in the finished work. It is the necessity of forms that develops within a work of art, more than the gilded frame or the edge of the proscenium arch, that separates the work of art from the world

For Marcuse, form is art's distinguishing characteristic. Form is not the shape given to content—it *is* content. Marcuse writes in *The Aesthetic Dimension*, "Aesthetic form is not opposed to content, not even dialectically. In the work of art, form becomes content and vice versa."[46] It is not clear to me why Marcuse abandons dialectics in his discussion of form and content. His position is easier to understand with respect to music than to art forms that are representational, such as the novel and much painting.

Whatever its relation to content, Marcuse is clear that there can be no art without form and no form without a boundary keeping life at bay. If form is abandoned, then art disappears into the maw of reality, and with it goes its promise:

> [R]enunciation of the aesthetic form is abdication of responsibility. It deprives art of the very form in which it can create that other reality within the established one—the cosmos of hope.[47]

Important as the concept of form may be for Marcuse, it remains elusive. In a footnote to a 1969 essay, "Art as Form of Reality," he writes:

> I shall use the term *Form* (capitalized) for that which defines Art as Art, that is to say, as essentially (ontologically) different not only from (everyday) reality but also from such other manifestations of intellectual culture as science and philosophy.[48]

So form is what defines art and art is defined by possessing form.

Two years earlier we find him using "form" not as what defines art, but as essentially synonymous with shape:

> What does Form actually accomplish? Form assembles, determines and bestows order on matter so as to give it an end. End in a literal sense, namely, to set definite limits within which the force of matter comes to rest within limits of accomplishment and fulfillment. . . . Form of a face, Form of a life, Form of a stone or a table but also form of a work of art. [49]

Marcuse may never have given a fully satisfactory explanation of the meaning of form in art, but he was adamant that it is by virtue of form that art achieves and maintains its autonomy vis-à-vis the dominant reality. Citing Hegel, he writes, "Art reduces the immediate contingencies in which an object (or totality of objects) exists to a state in which the object takes on the form and quality of freedom." [50] Paradoxically, the work of art can be a realm of freedom, because it submits to "a tyranny of form":

> [I]n an authentic work a necessity prevails which demands that no line, no sound could be replaced (in the optimal case, which doesn't exist). This inner necessity (the quality which distinguishes authentic from inauthentic works) is indeed tyranny in as much as it suppresses the immediacy of expression. But what is here suppressed is false

> immediacy: false to the degree to which it drags along the unreflected mystified reality."[51]

The tyranny of form frees art from the tyranny of externally imposed necessity, and therefore allows it to become a place where freedom reigns in a world that remains unfree:

> This submission to aesthetic form is the vehicle of the nonconformist sublimation which accompanies . . . desublimation. The ego and id, instinctual goals and emotions, rationality and imagination are withdrawn from their socialization by a repressive society and strive towards autonomy.[52]

Marcuse repeatedly rose in defense of form in art and identified the aesthetic dimension as the dimension in which we encounter that form. He saw form, and with it the aesthetic dimension, threatened from all sides: from elements in the new left and the old left for which form only has value as a delivery system for revolutionary content; from a counter-culture impatient with the instinctual sublimation that form requires; and finally from avant-gardes, which increasingly seemed bent on pushing art to the point where it turned on itself in an act of auto-cannibalism.

> We witness not only the political, but also, and primarily, the artistic attack on art in all its forms, on art as Form itself. The distance and dissociation of art from reality are denied, refused, and destroyed.[53]

All tendencies toward the disintegration of form and the breaching of the boundary with the world are threats to be resisted. He writes in *The Aesthetic Dimension*:

> Deliberate formless expression "banalizes" in as much as it obliterates the opposition to the established universe of discourse—an opposition which is crystallized in the aesthetic form.[54]

The abandonment of form is surrender to reality:

> When art abandons . . . autonomy and with it the aesthetic form in which the autonomy is expressed, art succumbs to that reality which it seeks to grasp and indict. . . . Anti-art is self-defeating from the outset.[55]

In *One-Dimensional Man,* Marcuse describes that merger as obscene:

> The obscene merger of aesthetics and reality refutes the philosophies which oppose "poetic" imagination to scientific and empirical Reason. . . . The archetypes of horror as well as of joy, of war as well as of peace lose their catastrophic character. . . . When technical progress cancels this separation . . . it also reduces the gap between imagination and Reason. The two antagonistic faculties become interdependent on common ground.[56]

Marcuse continued to defend form and the independence of the aesthetic dimension throughout his life, yet, at the same time, he saw that independence as both a strength and a weakness. Sealed off from life, art can only be a promise of pleasure, but it cannot fulfill that promise. Marcuse first explored this contradiction in an extraordinary essay written in 1937 on "The Affirmative Character of Culture." By affirmative culture he means "that culture of the bourgeois epoch, which led in the course of its own development to the segregation from civilization of the mental and spiritual world as an independent realm of value." Its "decisive characteristic," according to Marcuse, "is the assertion of a universally obligatory, eternally better and more valuable world essentially different from the factual world of the daily struggle for existence."[57]

By its willingness to coexist without challenging the realm of necessity, art, which is the quintessential expression of affirmative culture, "exonerated 'external conditions' . . . thus stabilizing their injustice. But it also held up to them as a task the image of a better order. The image is distorted. . . . Nevertheless it is an image of happiness."[58]

Art can only preserve the promise of happiness in an unhappy world by setting itself apart. "Affirmative culture," writes Marcuse, "was the historical form in which were preserved those human wants which surpassed the material reproduction of existence."[59] For centuries, perhaps millennia, human beings had assumed that those wants were beyond the possibility of fulfillment:

> Affirmative culture was the counterimage of an order in which the material reproduction of life left no space or time for those regions of existence which the ancients had designated as the "beautiful." It became customary to see the entire sphere of material reproduction as essentially tainted with a blemish of poverty, severity, and injustice and to abandon or suppress any demands protesting it.[60]

The abolition of so much want and suffering seemed like a utopian dream; it was impossible to imagine, except in dreams, that the world would ever be a peaceable kingdom, a garden of earthly delights. But those dreams never died, and in the '60s movements sprang up which believed in their fulfillment. In *Eros and Civilization*, Marcuse had argued that we were more repressed than necessary, and that material conditions were such that desire and civilization need not be in such conflict. Now political forces emerged that made the liberation of desire part of their political agenda.

Already in 1937, Marcuse could write: "The assertion that today culture has become unnecessary contains a dynamic, progressive element."[61] He envisaged a time when conditions would be such that the separation was no longer required:

> When culture gets to the point of having to sustain fulfillment itself and no longer merely desire, it will no longer be able to do so in contents that, as such, bear an affirmative character. . . . Beauty will find a new embodiment when it no longer is represented as real illusion but, instead, expresses reality and joy in reality. . . . Perhaps, however, beauty and its enjoyment will not even devolve upon art. Perhaps art as such will have no objects. For the common man it has been confined to museums for at least a century.[62]

In the '60s, Marcuse allowed himself for moments to believe that point had come. His belief waxed and waned with his assessment of the strength of the movements of liberation. In a 1967 lecture given at the School of Visual Arts in New York, Marcuse reflects that perhaps the time had come for a new relationship between art and life:

> [T]oday art, for the first time in history, is confronted with the possibility of entirely new modes of realization. Or the place of art in the world is changing, and art today is becoming a potential factor in the construction of a new reality, a prospect which would mean the cancellation *and* the transcendence of art in the fulfillment of its own end. [63]

Two years later, in his 1969 lecture, "Art as Form of Reality," Marcuse simultaneously acknowledges the validity of the desire to make art part of life, and warns against doing so before life itself had been transformed by revolution:

> [I]f art is still anything at all, it must be real, part and parcel of life—but of a life which is itself the conscious negation of the established way of life.[64]

In *An Essay on Liberation,* completed in 1968, he imagines that the end of art as an independent realm could come at that moment when the potential for radical transformation of society is finally realized. He entertains "the historical possibility of conditions in which the aesthetic could become a *gesellschaftliche Produktivkraft* [socially productive force] and as such could lead to the "end of art through its realization."[65] He does not see that possibility in the practice of social movements, but he believes it is within the reach of the resources made available by technology, should those resources be properly used:

> Today, the outline of such conditions appears only in the negativity of the advanced industrial societies. They are societies whose capabilities defy the imagination. No matter what sensibility art may wish to develop, no matter what Form it may wish to give to things, to life, no matter what vision it may wish to communicate—a radical change of experience is within the technical reaches of powers whose terrible imagination organizes the world in their own image and perpetuates, and ever bigger and better, the mutilated experience.[66]

Marcuse now sees the introduction into art of elements that are destructive of form not simply as a threat to be resisted, but as a sign that the time is right for art to break through its well-guarded boundary and join the fight against "repressive reason." "Non-objective, abstract paintings and sculpture, stream-of-consciousness and formless literature, twelve-tone composition, blues and jazz," he writes, represent "new modes of perception," which "dissolve the very structure of perception."[67]

> The fight is against the "Illusionistiche Kunst Europas": art must no longer be illusory because its relation to reality has changed: the latter has become susceptible to, even dependent on, the transforming function of art. The revolutions and the defeated and betrayed revolutions which occurred in the wake of the [First World] war denounced the reality which had made art and illusion, and in as much as art has been an illusion . . . the new art proclaims itself as anti-art.[68]

Here anti-art, art that is unwilling to remain an illusion, is seen as a sign that reality is "susceptible . . . to the transforming function of art."

This is Marcuse at his most optimistic. In 1977, when he published *The Aesthetic Dimension*, he no longer believed that any revolution in social conditions could fulfill the promise of art or render it obsolete. The promise of art would always and forever be illusory. He writes: "Art cannot redeem its promise, and reality offers no promises, only chances. We are back at the traditional concept of art as illusion (*Schein*), though perhaps beautiful illusion (*schöner Schein*)"[69]

Art is no longer "a potential factor in the construction of a new reality," nor is it any longer possible to imagine the prospect of "the cancellation *and* the transcendence of art in the fulfillment of its own end." Rather, art now is seen as a testament to the limits of the possibility of transformation in reality: "Art declares its *caveat* to the thesis according to which the time has come to change the world. While art bears witness to the necessity of liberation, it also testifies to its limits."[70] *The Aesthetic Dimension* is, as Marcuse suggest by his subtitle, a critique of Marxist aesthetics. Against orthodox Marxists he argues that the contradictions resolved in the aesthetic dimension will not be resolved in any possible socialist society:

> The institutions of a socialist society, even in their most democratic form, could never resolve all the conflicts between the universal and the particular, between human beings and nature, between individual and individual. . . . Here is the limit which drives the revolution beyond any accomplished stage of freedom: it is the struggle for the impossible, against the unconquerable whose domain can perhaps nevertheless be reduced.[71]

Reducing the "unconquerable" contradictions between human beings and between humanity and nature is the most one can hope for. Art becomes at the same time the custodian of a prophetic vision of a utopian goal toward which all revolutions advance and a caution that no revolution will ever reach that goal. It has one foot in the utopian future and another in the dystopian present.

If anything, reality is more dystopian today than it was when Marcuse was writing *The Aesthetic Dimension*. The collision between capitalism and nature appears to be unavoidable; the number of fatalities in that collision and the extent of collateral damage are unimaginable. Marcuse never questioned the value of art's promise of happiness, even as he lost faith that it could ever be anything more than just that—a promise. Whatever the state of the world, he held to the belief that art could continue to fashion that promise out of an intolerable reality. If the possibility of the end of art occured to him, it was a tabooed thought, suppressed, but pehaps, like all tabooed thoughts, never entirely extinguished.

Theodor Adorno famously denied the possibility of writing poetry after Auschwitz. "Cultural criticism," he wrote, "finds itself faced with the final stage of the dialectic of culture and barbarism. To write poetry after Auschwitz is barbaric. And this corrodes even the knowledge of why it has become impossible to write poetry today."[72] *

In *An Essay on Liberation*, Marcuse responded:

> Is it possible to write poetry after Auschwitz? The question has been countered: when the horror of reality tends to become total and blocks political action, where else than in the radical imagination, as refusal of reality, can the rebellion and its uncompromised goals be remembered?[73]

Eight years later Marcuse returned to the question in *The Aesthetic Dimension*:

> Auschwitz and My Lai, the torture, starvation, and dying . . . . Art draws away from this reality, because it cannot represent the suffering without subjecting it to aesthetic form, and thereby to the mitigating catharsis, to enjoyment. Art is inexorably infested with this guilt. Yet this does not release art from the necessity of recalling again and again that which can survive even Auschwitz and perhaps one day make it impossible. If even this memory were to be silenced, then the "end of art" would indeed have come.[74]

For a brief moment, the tabooed thought rises to the surface. Marcuse entertains the possibility of an "end of art," but only if the memory of "that which can survive even Auschwitz" is silenced. He does not dwell on the possibility. The thought is there—that the memory of what is good

* Later he thought better of denying future post-Auschwitz generations the consolation of poetry:

> "Perennial suffering has as much right to expression as the tortured have to scream; hence it may have been wrong to say that no poem could be written after Auschwitz."

(Theodor W. Adorno, *Negative Dialectics* "Part III. Models. Meditations on Metaphysics," trans. Dennis Redmond 1966, 354-357.)

and human and worth struggling for even after unspeakable atrocity could be extinguished—but as soon as it arises he moves on.

In "Art as Form of Reality," a 1969 lecutre delivered at the Guggenheim Museum in New York, he speculated that the disintegration of aesthetic form in avant-garde art might be a reflection of a reality that could no longer be redeemed by beauty.

> Harmonization of the beautiful and the true—what was supposed to make up the essential unity of the work of art has turned out to be an increasingly impossible *unification of opposites*, for the true has appeared as increasingly incompatible with the beautiful. Life, the human condition, has militated increasingly against the sublimation of reality in the Form of Art.[75]

The lecture was delivered the same year that Marcuse published *An Essay on Liberation*. In the *Essay* he had written that changes in reality were making it more "susceptible to the transforming function of art." In the lecture, he comes the opposite conclusion—reality is becoming less susceptible to that transformation. Did the waning of the energies of liberation movements, which reached their apogee in 1968 when the essay was probably written account for the shift in Marcuse's thinking? Marcuse never explored the unsettling implications of the idea that art might no longer be able to accomplish the aesthetic transformation of reality. No echo of it can be heard in *The Aesthetic Dimension* except for that one sentence about the silencing of memory.

Today the world is on the brink. What lies beyond the brink defies imagination. The tabooed thought of the end of art pushes past our resistance bringing with it unanswerable questions: Is art still possible? Can it remain a world apart in which form emerges out of freedom? Will it continue to preserve the promise of happiness?

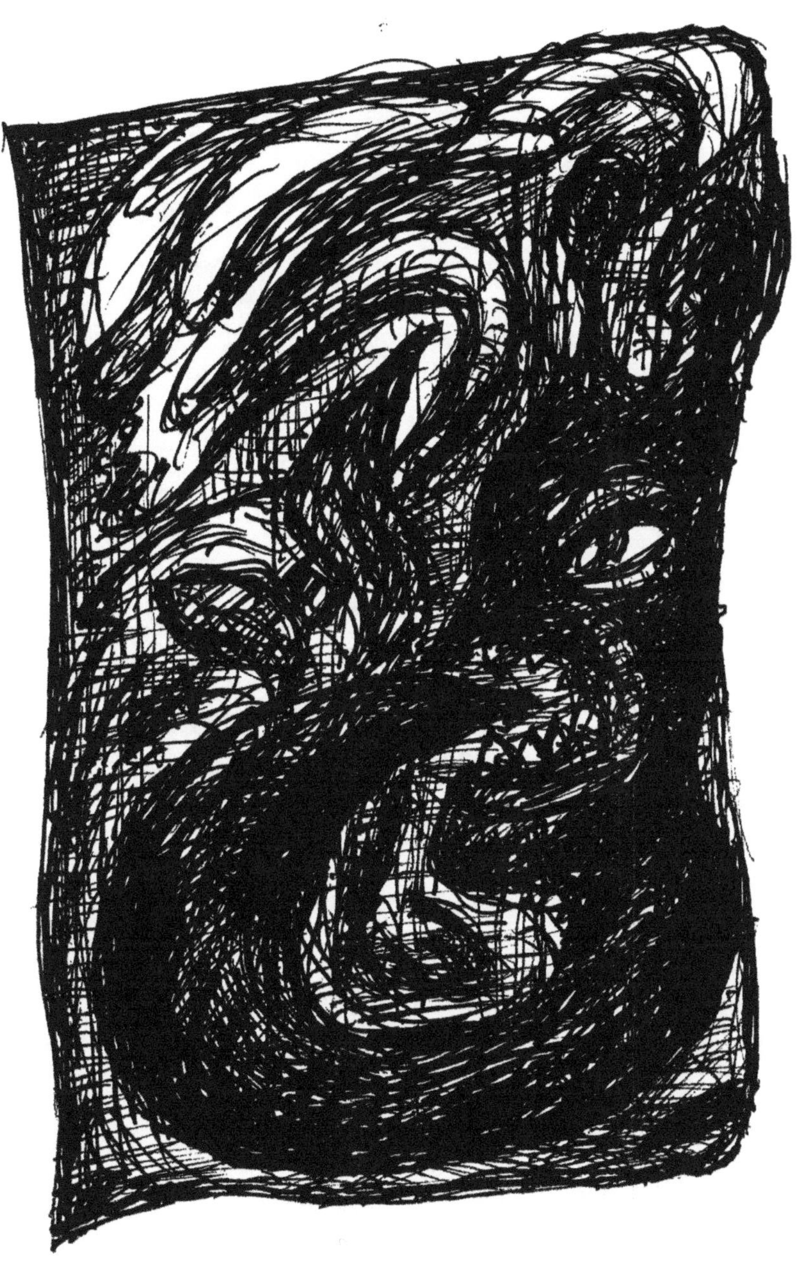

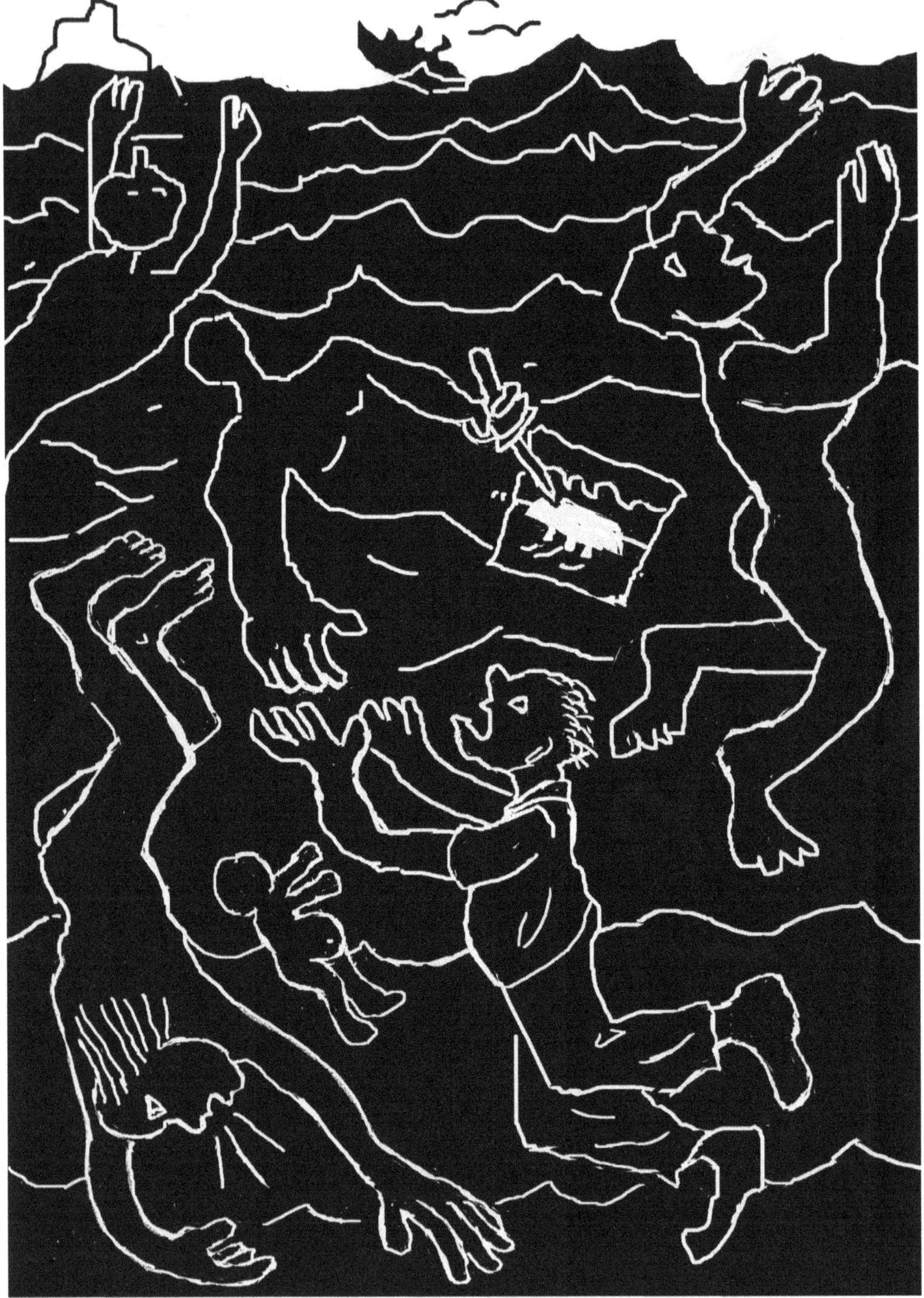

Notes

1. Tomkins, Calvin. "Missing in Action." *The New Yorker,* August 4, 2003, 43.

2. Van Gogh to Bernard, June 20, 1888, in Vincent van Gogh, *Letters to Emile Bernard,* ed. Douglas Lord. Museum of Modern Art, 1938, 39.

3. Ibid., 50.

4. Van Gogh to Theo, October 1885 in *The Complete Letters of Vincent Van Gogh,* Book II. Boston, Toronto, London: Little, Brown and Company, 428–429.

5. Van Gogh to Bernard, October 1888, in *Letters to Emile Bernard,* 90.

6. Van Gogh to Theo in *The Complete Letters of Vincent Van Gogh,* Book II, 401.

7. Van Gogh to Theo, 23 July 1890, found on his body after his death in *The Complete Letters of Vincent Van Gogh,* Book III. Boston, Toronto, London: Little, Brown and Company, 298.

8. *The Return of the Buddha: The Quingzhou Discoveries.* London: Royal Academy of Arts, 2002, 23.

9. Janheinz Jahn, *Muntu: The New African Culture.* New York: Grove Press, 1961, 157-158.

10. Sylvia Ardyn Boone, *Radiance from the Waters: Ideals of Feminine Beauty in Mende Art.* New Haven and London: Yale University Press, 1986, 157.

11. Ibid., 158.

12. Andre Malraux, *The Metamorphoses of the Gods,* trans. Stuart Gilbert (Doubleday & Co.: Garden City, New York, 1960) 33.

13. Boone, *Radiance from the Waters,* 426.

14. Charles Baudelaire, *Eugene Delacroix, Work and Life.* New York: Lear Publishers, 1947, 63-64.

15. From Courbet's letter responding to his students requesting he teach, December 25, 1861. Quoted in Getty Museum website at http://www.getty.edu/art/collections/bio/a369-1.html

16. "Claude Monet-The Rouen Cathedral Series-the Climax of Impressionism." theartwolf.com, online art magazine, http://www.theartwolf.com/monet_cathedral.htm

17. "In July 1875 Monet's wife had fallen seriously ill; yet neither her illness nor the continuous threats of his landlord could prevent him from working. And when Camille eventually died he noticed, in spite of all his grief, as he contemplated her at daybreak, that his eyes perceived more than anything else the different colorations of her young face. Even before he had decided to retain for a last time her likeness, his painter's instinct had seen the blue, yellow, and gray tonalities cast by death. With horror he felt himself a prisoner of his visual experiences and compared his lot to that of the animal which turns the millstone."

John Rewald, *The History of Impressionism*. New York: The Museum of Modern Art, 1946, 292.

18. http://www.theartwolf.com/monet_cathedral.htm

19. Maurice Merleau-Ponty, *Cézanne's Doubt*. University of Massachusetts Lowell, 3, http://faculty.uml.edu/rinnis/cezannedoubt.pdf, [acessed January 8, 2014]

20. Cézanne to Bernard in Paul Cézanne, *Letters*, ed. John Rewald. New York: DeCapo Press, 1974.

21. Cézanne to Bernard, April 15, 1904, in Paul Cézanne, *Letters*, 301.

22. Joachim Gasquet, *Joachim Gasquet's Cézanne: A Memoir with Conversations*. London: Thames and Hudson, 1991, 163-164.

23. The move towards art that is "impressionistic" has a long history in the West: a continuous line can be traced from the Gothic to Impressionism comparable to the line leading from late medieval economy to high capitalism, and modern man, who regards his whole existence as a struggle and a competition, who translates all being into motion and change, for whom experience of the world increasingly becomes experience of time.

Arnold Hauser, *A Social History of Art*. London: Routledge & Kegan Paul, 1951, 872.

24. Karl Marx, *Economic and Philosophic Manuscripts of 1844*, trans. Martin Milligan. Amherst, New York: Prometheus Books, 1988, 71.

25. Patrick Marnham, *Dreaming with His Eyes Open: A Life of Diego Rivera.* New York: Knopf, 131.

26. Diego Rivera with Gladys March, *My Art, My Life.* New York: Citadel Press, 1960, 124.

27. "Surrealism, as I envisage it, asserts our absolute *nonconformism* so clearly that there can be no question of claiming it as witness when the real world comes up for trial." André Breton, "First Surrealist Manifesto," 1924 in *Surrealists on Art,* ed. Lucy R. Lippard. Engelwood Cliffs: Prentice Hall, 1970, 27.

28. "Surrealism was not afraid to make for itself a tenet of total revolt, complete insubordination, of sabotage according to rule, and why it still expects nothing safe from violence. The simplest surrealist act consists of dashing down into the street, pistol in hand, and firing blindly, as fast as you can pull the trigger, into the crowd. Anyone who, at least once in his life, has not dreamed of thus putting an end to the petty system of debasement and cretinization in effect has a well-defined place in that crowd, with his belly at barrel level." (In a footnote, Breton faces to defend himself without admitting that he is doing so: "As for that act that I term the simplest: it is clear that my intention is not to recommend it above every other because it is simple.") André Breton, "Second Surrealist Manifesto," 1929 in *Surrealists on Art,* ed. Lucy R. Lippard. Engelwood Cliffs: Prentice Hall, 1970, 29.

29. André Breton, "What Is Surrealism?" 1934 in *What Is Surrealism: Selected Writings*, ed. Frank Rosemont. New York: Monad Press, 1978, 113.

30. David Alfaro Siqueiros, "A Declaration of Social, Political, and Aesthetic Principles," 1922, drafted and signed by members of the Syndicate of Technical Workers, Painters and Sculptors in David A. Siqueiros, *Art and Revolution.* London: Lawrence and Wishart, 1975, 24-25.

31. Rivera, *My Art, My Life*, 287.

32. "Statement of Frida Kahlo," Appendix, *Rivera My Art, My Life,* 303.

33. Jose Clemente Orozco, *An Autobiography,* trans. Robert C, Stephenson. Mineola, New York: Dover Publications, Inc., 2001, 40.

34. John Palmer Leeper, Introduction, Jose Clemente Orozco, *An Autobiography,* trans. Robert C, Stephenson. Mineola. New York: Dover Publications, Inc., 2001, xxi.

35. Ibid., 93-94.

36. Leticia Alvarez, "The Influence of the Mexican Muralists in the United States: From the New Deal to the Abstract Expressionism," 36. http://scholar.lib.vt.edu/theses/available/etd-05092001-130514/unrestricted/thesis.pdf.

37. Ibid., 36.

38. Ibid., 46.

39. Walter Benjamin, "Art in the Age of Mechanical Reproduction," *Illuminations.* New York: Schocken Books, 1969, 211.

40. Jonathan Good, "How Many Photos Have Ever Been Taken?" http://blog.1000memories.com/94-number-of-photos-ever-taken-digital-and-analog-in-shoebox. Another commentator estimated 250 billion photographs were made in 2007 and that by 2010 the yearly production will rise to half a trillion photographs annually. (Francis Richard "Photography's Ghosts: The Image and Its Artifice," *The Nation,* March 16, 2009, 32, citing Fred Ritchin, *After Photography,* W.W. Norton & Co., 2008.)

41. "Evo Morales Opens Climate Change Conference in Tiquipaya," Democracy Now, radio broadcast, April 21, 2010.

42. Fredric Jameson, "The Antinomies of Post Modernity" in *The Cultural Turn: Selected Writings on the Postmodern, 1983–1998.* London: Verso, 1998, 50.

43. *National Geographic News*, "Oldest Jewelry Found in Moroccan Cave," June 7, 2007. http://news.nationalgeographic.com/news/pf/12023616.html.

44. Van Gogh to Bernard, June 1888, in *Letters to Emile Bernard,* ed. Douglas Lord. Museum of Modern Art, 1938, 45.

45. Van Gogh to Theo, May 20, 1888 (489) in *The Complete Letters of Vincent Van Gogh,* Book II, 570.

46. Herbert Marcuse, *The Aesthetic Dimension.* Boston: Beacon Press, 1978, 41.

47. Marcuse, *The Aesthetic Dimension,* 52.

48. Herbert Marcuse, "Art as Form of Reality," *Art and Liberation: Collected Papers of Herbert Marcuse,* Volume 4, ed. Douglas Kellner. London and New York: Routledge, 2007, 141.

49. Herbert Marcuse, "Art in the One-Dimensional Society," *Art and Liberation: Collected Papers of Herbert Marcuse,* Volume 4, ed. Douglas Kellner. London and New York: Routledge, 2007, 119-120.

50. Herbert Marcuse, *One-Dimensional Man.* Boston: Beacon Press, 1964, 239.

51. Marcuse, *The Aesthetic Dimension,* 42-43.

52. Ibid., 43-44

53. Marcuse, "Art as Form of Reality," 140.

54. Marcuse, *The Aesthetic Dimension,* 43.

55. Ibid., 49.

56. *One-Dimensional Man,* 248-249.

57. Herbert Marcuse, "The Affirmative Character of Culture," trans. Jeremy Shapiro (originally published in German in 1937) in *Art and Liberation: Collected Papers of Herbert Marcuse*, Volume 4, ed. Douglas Kellner. London and New York Routledge, 2007, 87.

58. Ibid., 104

59. Ibid.

60. Ibid., 110.

61. Ibid., 111.

62. Ibid.

63. Marcuse, "Art in the One-Dimensional Society," 116.

64. Marcuse, "Art as Form of Reality," 140.

65. Herbert Marcuse, *An Essay on Liberation.* Boston: Beacon Press, 1969, 45.

66. Ibid.

67. Ibid., 38.

68. Ibid., 41.

69. Marcuse, *The Aesthetic Dimension,* 48.

70. Ibid., 68.

71. Ibid., 71–72.

72. Theodor Adorno, "Cultural Criticism and Society," written in 1949, first published in 1951, and collected in *Prisms.* Cambridge, Massachusetts: MIT Press, 1986, 34.

73. Marcuse, *An Essay on Liberation.* Boston: Beacon Press, 1969, 44–45.

74. Marcuse, *The Aesthetic Dimension.* Boston: Beacon Press, 1977, 55–56.

75. Marcuse, "Art as Form of Reality," 143.

Index

www.ingramcontent.com/pod-product-compliance
Lightning Source LLC
LaVergne TN
LVHW021127160826
845679LV00015B/1672

* 9 7 8 0 9 9 0 4 9 6 9 0 8 *